GETTING KIDS STARTED

IN ARTS AND CRAFTS

Also by the Author:

129 Art Lessons in 26 Media

Lois Ellen Eben

GETTING KIDS STARTED IN ARTS AND CRAFTS

Illustrations by the Author

Parker Publishing Company, Inc.   West Nyack, New York

Library of Congress Cataloging in Publication Data
Eben, Lois Ellen, 1922-
Getting Kids started in arts and crafts.
Includes index.
1. Art—Study and teaching (Elementary)—
United States. 2. Perceptual learning. I. Title.
N362.E2   372.5'044   81-14213
ISBN 0-13-354696-9 AACR2

DEDICATION

This book is dedicated to the numerous teachers who are striving to help children learn and develop as wholesome, intelligent individuals, in whom there is a love both of freedom and of The Arts.

It is especially dedicated to Frances H. Kinkle and Mary Lou Webster who belong to that elite group.

Special thanks go to Louis and Ellen Eben for their understanding and beautiful love.

A WORD FROM THE AUTHOR

"Dr. Eben, I have a tummy ache," said the child. Nodding sympathetically, I told her I knew some magic. I rubbed the tiny abdomen, at the same time saying some imaginary, mystical words. Then I asked how she felt. She thought for a minute, and assured me, "I feel better. It's all gone."

My students have always expected me, as an art teacher, to be able to perform the impossible, whether the problem is to glue a sole back on a shoe, mend a broken toy, wash paint out of a new pair of pants, or rub a tummy. However, these are only a part of my job.

In addition to teaching (and other RELATED activities), I perform two very important functions.

1. I plan experiences that promote growth and development in and through art. The core of my curriculum is planned for the needs of the children who will be using it. I get them started, in the early elementary grades, with an introduction to arts and crafts that uses experiences predominantly in the sensory, developmental and design areas. Each lesson is formulated to meet both the generalized needs of the class and the individualized requirements of each child.

2. I am constantly asked to recommend and demonstrate art activities that can be done in the classroom, with the regular classroom teacher instructing.

This book will present answers for both of these needs. The experiences shown will include the basic art activities and media required for children in the primary grades (K-3) and suggestions will be given for their extended use throughout the elementary years. (Beginning with the simple experiences of exploring and manipulating the media, children work gradually toward refinement, and then to the more complex skills and techniques as they grow older.)

6

This book has been written for the use of both elementary art and classroom teachers, and especially for:

1. Those looking for new ideas or new ways of using materials which will bring out inventiveness, creativity and originality.

2. Those seeking early developmental experiences.

3. Those who lack formal art training.

4. Those who need self-assurance in working with art activities.

5. Those in a limited-budget setting.

6. Those who need special enrichment activities for the artistically gifted child.

It is composed of twelve chapters, each presenting practical, enjoyable and challenging activities. The first chapter is devoted to introductory experiences for the child who has had little or no exposure to arts and crafts. It consists of very basic, developmental projects. The remaining eleven chapters are designed to nurture the child's ability to:

1. Show imagination, inventiveness, and originality through two-dimensional and three-dimensional creative expression.

2. Bring together personal emotions, imagination, and intellect in order to solve problems and think independently.

3. See, feel, hear, smell, taste and understand these sensations.

4. Use line, shape, texture, color and space according to simple design principles.

5. Experience a sense of accomplishment, self-pride and worthiness through the use of art media.

6. Handle art tools and materials skillfully and efficiently.

7. Be able to work independently, as well as with one's peers.

8. Learn about artists as well as art skills and techniques.

It is my hope that this book will help children get started in arts and crafts, and that it will nourish their inventiveness, creativity and originality so that these qualities will become a permanent part of their personalities.

LOIS ELLEN EBEN

TABLE OF CONTENTS

GENERAL PREPARATIONS

Play It Safe . . . . . Be Prepared!

Planning and preparation are absolute necessities for art activities. These periods can be chaotic if one is not ready. For this reason, the following suggestions will help *BEFORE AND AFTER THE LESSON PROCEDURES.*

1. Always have adequate washing facilities (soap, towels, and sponges) at the sink. If the classroom doesn't have a sink, basins or pails of water will do nicely. They're definitely not "luxury class," but what can one do in these days of budget crunches?

2. Children should be covered with a smock, apron or old shirt, with sleeves rolled up, preferably.

3. All art work should be adequately labeled with the child's name to prove ownership.

A. Make your own name tags by punching a hole in a card, inserting string in the hole, and tying onto each piece of sculpture.

B. Write names on masking tape and place underneath the art work.

C. Write names on papers to be used for drawing, painting, and fingerpainting. Often it is best to do this on the underside BEFORE the activities begin. This is the teacher's responsibility when the children are very young.

4. All working and storage surfaces should be thoroughly covered with one or more layers of newspaper or scrap plastic, such as old shower curtains or garbage bags.

5. Provide a safe storage place for all finished and unfinished work. Storage requires that pieces will be easy to locate, and take up as little space as possible. Placing a painting on the floor may result in children walking on wet paintings . . . and irate custodians. Instead, dry your paintings by clipping to the window blinds, tacking onto a bulletin board, or taping to the wall with masking tape, which should not mar the surface. Also, a rope, wire or cord can be strung across the room. Wet paintings can be attached to this line with clothespins, clamps or special clips. NEVER HANG OVER CHILDREN'S HEADS, BOOKS OR SUPPLIES.

6. Three dimensional, and freshly glued work as well as all painted or glazed sculpture, must have adequate space so that pieces will not touch each other. Clay sculptures require a safe, slow, drying area, never in the hot sun, or over a heater.

7. Collect containers of various kinds and sizes. These can be used to hold water, paint, glue and other art materials. Especially useful are: plastic egg boxes; margarine tubs, with tops; aluminum pie and cake tins; juice cans; small jars with large openings at the top; and cut-down gallon water, milk or bleach bottles.

Introductory Exposure to the Arts and Crafts

PART
1

1

Developmental Experiences
for the Young Child

Arts and crafts experiences are basic to the growth of the boy and girl in the elementary school. Hands gain strength! Muscular control is developed!

This chapter, therefore, introduces art in the elementary school through the use of manipulative activities. Introductory routines as well as the names of art materials, colors, and tools are presented. The joy and emotional appeal of the visual arts will become apparent to the child as he or she works with paint and paper. Even the soles of shoes will be used for a printing experience. Action activities will be given using wood, chalk, paint and clay, and little bodies will become a part of the art process.

LESSON 1: COVER IT WITH PAINT!
SIMPLE PAINTING EXPERIENCES

Watch a child's face as he mixes two colors of paint together. When he discovers a new color, you'll see (and sometimes hear) pure ecstasy! Watch his actions, too, and see how his body is affected by his painting.

Tools, Material and Equipment:

Powdered tempera paint	Newspaper
Large brushes	Boxes
Water container	Paper towels
Egg boxes	Cylinders
Newsprint paper	

Preparation:

Suggest that children collect boxes, cylinders and egg boxes. As the collection grows, have the children compare them, what they were used for, how they could be utilized, and discuss size and shape. "This box is very small. This one is large. Those are curved sides. These cylinders are longer than those cylinders."

Regarding the number of items to be collected, it is suggested that one egg box, plus three other pieces, will be adequate for each child.

Cover the tables with newspaper and give each child an egg box. Using paint only in the primary colors, i.e., red, yellow and blue; place one-half teaspoon of each in three of the sections of the box. The other nine sections can be utilized for mixing colors. (Figure 1-1.)

Partially fill margarine tubs with water for cleaning brushes and adding water to dry paint. Young children spill less if the container is fairly large and has a well-balanced base. (Figure 1-2.)

If the children are working on tables, one water container will be sufficient for four children to share.

1-1

1-2

Developmental Procedure for Activity

Give children large brushes and the freedom to experiment with them. (As they become adept at using them, small brushes can be added.)

Allow them to select a box or cylinder that they would like to decorate. (As one is finished, a second may be used, and then a third, if time permits and interest is sustained.)

Discuss the use of primary colors. They're bright and beautiful and are the most important. They're called primary because all kinds of new colors may be made from these three.

Demonstrate how the brush is dipped into the water. Then place a few drops of water into the dry paint and mix. (Never pour it in.) (Figure 1-3.) Mix one color at a time, wash the brush, and then mix another. Use only enough water to make the paint smooth and moist. Now begin to paint, filling in all the spaces with rich, beautiful color.

1-3

Whenever a new color is used, the brush must be cleaned by:

1. Wiping off the excess paint on a paper towel.
2. Dipping into water and swishing around.
3. Drying off on newspaper (on the table) or a paper towel.

When the brush is clean, the colors are kept pure and bright.

When the painting activity has been completed, the brush must again be thoroughly cleaned, after which it should be placed in a container with the bristle end up.

Allow the objects to dry before they are taken home. Children are usually very excited over these first painting experiences and will never want to wait, but BE FIRM, for mothers are not tolerant of wet paint on cars, clothes, and furniture.

Specific Skills and Concepts To Be Learned:

1. Mixing powdered, tempera paint.
2. Painting with primary colors.
3. Mixing new colors from primaries.
4. Cleaning and storing paint brushes.
5. Comparison of size and shape.

Adaptations:

This lesson may be utilized with all the elementary grades as (a) a preliminary to a painting unit or (b) a "refresher" on mixing and caring for simple painting materials. In addition, upper elementary children can be given the following painting problems:

1. Paint with thin tempera over a crayon design, which has previously been applied to the boxes or cylinders. (Crayon must be applied heavily or paint will cover it.) (Figure 1-4.)

2. Paint papier-maché egg boxes in the primary colors. Then attach them, by stapling, to the bulletin board. This is called a relief sculpture. (Figure 1-5.)

3. Glue cardboard boxes together to make a box sculpture. Then paint as desired. (Figure 1-6.)

1-4

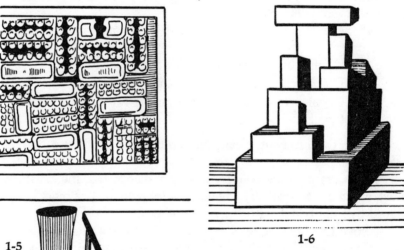

1-5

1-6

Lesson 2. Two-Fisted Painting!
Finger painting with Two Hands

Tools, Materials and Equipment:

Finger paint, commercial or:	Soap and towels
Classroom finger paint, using wallpaper paste and powdered tempera paint	Finger-paint paper
	Quart container
	Pint containers
	Newspapers
Basin of water	Sponges

Preparation:

Always make the necessary preliminary preparations for finger painting. IT MUST BE WELL PLANNED.

As stated previously in "General Preparations," write the children's names on the dull side of the finger paint paper, cover everything (except the children) with newspapers. Cover the children with smocks or a reasonable substitute. Roll up all sleeves. Know where the completed, WET, STICKY paintings will be stored. Have PLENTY of towels available, with soap and water accessible WITHIN the classroom.

Prepare finger paint. Finger paint comes in various forms: moist, dry and classroom-made. One type of the classroom-made variety is described below:

1. Mix a quart of wallpaper paste with water, using the directions given by the manufacturer of the paste.
2. Divide into four equal (½ cup) portions. Put each portion into a pint-sized jar.
3. Place one tablespoon of powdered tempera in each jar, replace top on jar, and shake until the color is well integrated with the paste. If color is too pale, add more paint.
4. Each jar can be made into a different color of finger paint. A good beginning set of colors would be: red, yellow, blue and green.
5. Allow children to help mix the paint.

Developmental Procedure for Activity:

Introduce finger-painting with a demonstration.

Hold up a piece of finger-paint paper. Point out that it is shiny on one side, for the purpose of allowing the paint to be easily smoothed over the paper with the hands. The paper is dull on the other side.

Place shiny side up. Dip a sponge into water and squeeze some water on top of the paper. Spread the water over the entire surface with your hand.

Now place some finger paint in the center and, using your hands, work it out to the edges. Be certain there is enough paint and moisture together on the paper as you spread the paint. If

not, add more. Keep the surface moist and the color bright.
(Figure 1-7.)

Finger paint is used to make patterns or designs.
Demonstrate how to do it with hands, fingers and palm of
hand. Then try it with two fists at the same time. (Figure 1-8.)

1-8

1-7

Let children experiment with these techniques. Stress that
this is neither a drawing nor a writing activity. It's a method of
making rhythmical designs. Experiment. Make twin designs
with two hands going at the same time. Feel the smoothness . . .
. . the coolness . . . . . and the wetness! Emphasize big
movements with those TWO FISTS. Try for unusual effects.

When completed, place the paintings in a safe storage area,
making certain that none are overlapping another painting, for
finger paint sticks together better than some glues.

Specific Skills and Concepts To Be Learned:

1. Making finger paint.
2. Using finger paint.
3. Applying paint to a surface with one's hands.
4. Creating designs with two hands, used simultane-
   ously.

Adaptations:

All elementary school children enjoy using finger paint. However, the experiences for older children should include more utilitarian products. Try utilizing finger-painted paper as follows:

1. For book covers.

2. For gift wrapping paper.

3. Cut out shapes from the finger-painted paper and glue onto construction paper for a lesson in design.

4. Use the finger-painted paper as a background for a realistic picture, drawing on top of it with crayons, oil pastels or felt markers.

LESSON 3. DANCE WITH FINGER PAINT!
FINGER PAINTING WITH COMBS, TOOTHBRUSHES, AND UNUSUAL SURFACES

Finger-painting is a rhythmic experience. Bring some music into the classroom, via the record player, and watch the children's hands dance with finger paint. Let them do the "Finger-paint Crickleditz."

Tools, Materials and Equipment:

Record player
Finger paint
Newspapers
Basin of water
Soap
Paper towels

Records
Finger-paint paper
Sponges
Creative tools (combs,
    toothbrushes, forks,
    spools)
Various background surfaces

Preparation:

This lesson is a continuation of the last lesson. The procedures outlined previously should be followed.

Set up a record player, with some lively music on it.

Developmental Procedure for Activity:

Demonstrate and allow children to work as follows:

Apply paint to paper and spread out smoothly. Use various tools to make designs on the paint. Try toothbrushes, combs, sponges, rolled up cloth, cotton swabs, plastic forks, spools, sticks and even plastic knives. Let the comb make a wavy design across the paper. Introduce the children to the Crickleditz: the finger painting dance. Crickleditz with the comb, or use a fork to dance with. (Figure 1-9.)

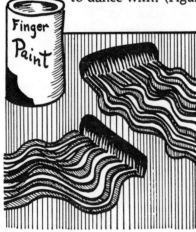

1-9

Drag the tools across the paper over the paint. Make repeated, rhythmic designs from one side to the other. Keep time, of course, with the music. Let your hands feel the rhythm. Let it come out of your hands onto the paper, and DO THE CRICKLEDITZ.

As an additional experience, experiment with finger paint on various kinds of paper. Use construction paper (which absorbs the paint). Try shiny backgrounds such as foils or metallics. What happens if you use plasticized paper? or wallpaper? or paper towels? What happens if you finger paint on wood? or cardboard? This kind of an activity teaches about textures, or the surface qualities of objects, i.e., how they feel.

Specific Skills and Concepts To Be Learned:

1. Finger painting can be done on various surfaces.
2. It is a rhythmic and feeling experience.
3. Tools can be utilized to create designs on finger paint.

Adaptations:

Middle and upper grades may wish to work with the following more complex activities:

1. Make a print by placing a second sheet of paper on top of the wet finger-painted design. Press down and quickly pull apart. This makes a duplicate print with slightly less paint on it. (Figure 1-10.)

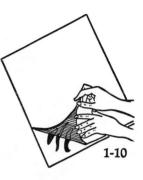

1-10

2. Make soap paint with detergent, starch and powdered paint or food coloring. Soap paint is similar to finger paint. Mix together one-half cup liquid starch and two cups of detergent. An electric mixer gives the paint a smoother consistency. Color the paint by adding powdered tempera or food coloring.

LESSON 4: STAMP THOSE SHOES! PRINTING WITH THE SOLES OF SHOES

A little boy once brought his old sneakers to school, thinking his art teacher could make use of everything. He was correct, for the soles of sneakers, or shoes, make excellent printing devices.

Tools, Materials and Equipment:

Old shoes or sneakers	Crayons
Tempera paint	Brushes
Juice cans	Sponges
Newspapers	Basins
Large mural paper	Felt markers

Preparation:

Lay out large sheets of paper on a long table or a row of desks. Cover floor with newspapers.

Put tempera paint in juice cans (about half full). Each table will require a set of colors (red, yellow, blue, orange, purple, and green). Two old sneakers or shoes with a pattern on their soles, are adequate for each mural. It is suggested that four to six children work on a mural. The rest of the class can watch as each group works, or all can work at the same time (if teacher has plenty of aspirin on hand).

Developmental Procedure for Activity:

Begin the lesson by holding up a few shoes or sneakers. Explain the difference between the various kinds of soles, looking at the design on the surface of each. Discuss the reason for these imprints.

Demonstrate on the board by painting a sole with water.

1. Make a row of wet sole patterns across the board. (Figure 1-11.)

2. Make a row with a sole pointed upward, and a sole pointed downward. (Figure 1-12.)

3. Use two different soles together. (Figure 1-13.)

4. Scatter the design all over the paper, or chalkboard.

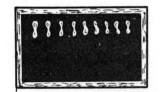

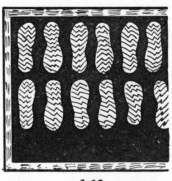

1-12

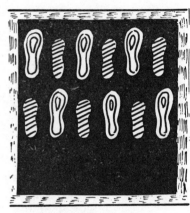

1-13

1-11

Now paint a thin layer of tempera over the surface of the sole and press down onto a piece of newspaper. Press from heel to toe and from toe to heel. (Figure 1-14.)

1-14

Begin working on the mural paper with children cooperating and taking turns, unless each has a shoe to use. Decide what colors to use. How will they combine their colors? Different ones can be painted on the same shoe, but the surface will have to be wiped clean if brilliant colors are wanted. Exciting effects can be obtained if some color is left in the lower surfaces of the sole and a new color is painted on the ridges. Try out many different ways of stamping the designs onto the paper. Colors may be overlapped if desired, but the children will need to wait until one color is dry before applying another.

While the children are working, tell them a mural is a decoration for a wall or a ceiling, and can be made from all kinds of materials, such as paint, clay, stones, tiles, paper and metal. Has any one ever seen a mural? Where? Have you seen any famous murals?

After the children are satisfied with the number of stamped sole patterns, suggest that they fill in the background in some way by (a) painting in one solid color (Figure 1-15) or (b) drawing lines around each pattern using felt markers, paint brushes, or heavy crayons. (Figure 1-16.)

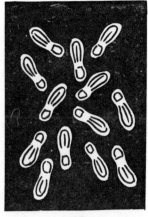

1-15

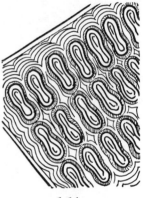

1-16

Specific Skills and Concepts To Be Learned:

1. Design is all around us, waiting to be discovered.
2. Murals are wall decorations.
3. Patterns may be repeated.
4. Backgrounds are a part of the design and should, therefore, be filled in.

Adaptations:

This idea may be adapted to other types of mural making, such as:

1. Paint the wheels of a bicycle and ride it across the mural paper.

2. Paint sponges and stamp a sponge pattern.

3. Use the "stamp a sole" idea. Then trace the feet of each child in the classroom on construction paper. Cut them out and glue onto the mural to give a shadow effect.

4. Upper grade students may make linoleum blocks of sneaker designs, or pictures of sneakers. These, then, can be stamped into a mural.

LESSON 5: CAN YOU CUT A SHAPE?
CUT PAPER DESIGNS

Paper cutting requires muscle control. While mastery of this skill is achieved through continuous practice, there are some children who acquire this ability much more quickly than others. Some have muscles that are better developed when they arrive in kindergarten. All will need much encouragement in their efforts!

Tools, Materials and Equipment:

Scissors	Tissue paper
Paste	Construction paper
Old magazines	Newspapers
String	Catalogs

Preparation:

Collect old magazines and the colored sections from newspapers. Catalogs are useful, too.

Obtain the best possible scissors, having an assortment that includes:

1. Left-handed scissors
2. Small, sharp teachers' scissors
3. Large classroom scissors
4. Pinking and scalloping scissors

Young children usually begin to cut by snipping with the ends of the scissors. (They snip along the paper's edge.) Some hold the scissors in such a way that they crease the paper, without actually making a cut. Left-handed children have many problems in cutting, even with the use of special left-handed scissors. Then, there is the problem of the right-handed child who tries to use left-handed scissors. THEY ALL NEED PRACTICE AND ENCOURAGEMENT UNDER A WATCHFUL TEACHER.

If the children are well disciplined with regard to sitting, and not walking around the room, a small, sharp, better quality pair of scissors will be of great help in learning to cut. In fact, much of the problem is with the *scissors* and not with the child.

Developmental Procedure for Activity:

Encourage practice by having the children cut:

1. Small scraps into smaller scraps.
2. Colored shapes from old magazines or catalogs.
3. Circles, squares, and triangles.

These cut shapes can be arranged on construction paper in any way. Stress the correct use of paste as an adhesive, not a "painting" material.

Next have the children practice cutting strips of paper so that they can cut in a straight line. (Figure 1-17.)

Cut photographs from newspapers and magazines. Cut around the edges of these pictures.

Combine strips and photographs by pasting together, making a hanging design. (Figure 1-18.)

Show children how to cut strips and bend back and forth to make simple springs. These can be added to the hanging design. (Figure 1 - 19.)

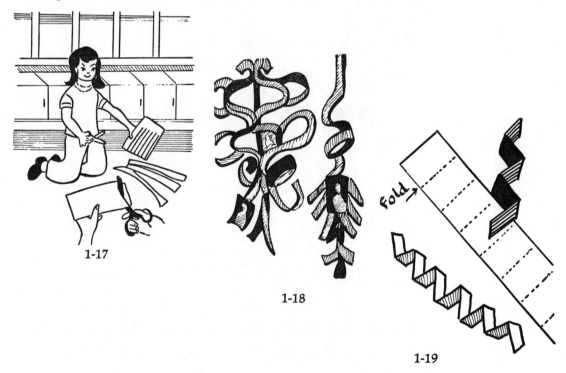

1-17

1-18

1-19

1-20

After much practice, and when children are able to cut fairly well, give them a more difficult experience. Using tissue paper, cut out balloons. Paste them all over a construction paper background. Add small pieces of string to make the balloons look more realistic. (Figure 1-20.)

While working with paper, scissors and paste, very young children should be encouraged to:

1. Use scissors safely and correctly.
2. Keep all scraps off the floor, picking up those that fall IMMEDIATELY.
3. Use paste correctly—not too much and not too little.

Another hard process for little children is the tearing of paper. It is extremely hard to do but after acquiring some facility with the use of scissors, practice with tearing is suggested.

Tear paper leaves in autumn colors and long strips of brown (for trunk). Paste these together in the form of a tree on a construction paper background. Ground and sky may be added. (Figure 1-21.)

1-21

Specific Skills and Concepts To Be Learned:

1. There are different kinds of scissors.
2. Paper can be cut with scissors and torn with one's fingers.

3. Scissors are a dangerous tool and must be used wisely.
4. Paper can be pasted together, or onto a background.
5. There are different thicknesses of paper.

Adaptations:

Older elementary school children may wish to work with cut and torn paper as follows:

1. Use pinking or scalloping scissors to create unusual edges to the cut paper. This is also very effective on greeting cards.
2. Create greeting cards with torn paper shapes.
3. Discover the mysteries of various colors, thicknesses, textures of different kinds of papers, by using them in two-dimensional and three-dimensional pictures.

LESSON 6. SANDPAPER SOME SMOOTH WOOD! GLUED WOODEN SCULPTURE

Wood presents many challenges. It's fun to use, easy to glue, and wooden sculptures made by very young children can be quite attractive. The making of a wooden sculpture is excellent for the development of manual coordination and dexterity, and helps the child's sense of balance, too.

Tools, Materials and Equipment:

White glue
Paint brushes
Tempera paint
Margarine tubs, with
  and without lids

Wood scraps
Sandpaper, medium
Spray paint

Preparation:

Collect wooden scraps. These can be obtained free-of-charge from cooperative lumberyards, parents and/or school custodians. If there is a cabinet maker in the area, his scraps are especially beautiful. There are pieces cut in curves, different kinds and tones of wood, imperfect knobs and handles, and other unusual shapes.

Old broom handles can be sawed into sections of various sizes. Dowels, popsicle sticks, used matches, toothpicks, tongue depressors, and spools add interest to a wooden construction. Also necessary are some fairly large, flat pieces of wood (or heavy cardboard) for the base. These should be no smaller than 6" x 6", but preferably larger. One piece per child is required.

Inspect all wood, before it is turned over to the children, to see that there are no nails in it, no sharp points, or rough splinters.

Prepare the glue by pouring a small amount into margarine tubs. Replace the lid on the container to keep the glue from drying out. Incidentally, these can be used again and again, as long as the lids fit the containers.

Developmental Procedure for Activity:

Talk about sandpaper. How does it feel? What is it used for? Give each child a piece and ask him to feel the roughness.

Show a piece of wood that has an interesting grain in it. What is the grain in wood? How does it get there? Discuss the tree's rings of growth. ((Figure 1-22.) Demonstrate the method of sanding wood. Sand all sides, sanding with the grain, trying to make it nice and smooth. Beware of splinters and rough edges.

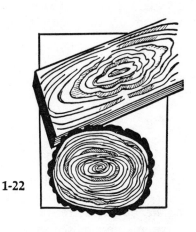

1-22

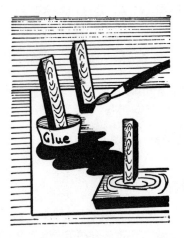

1-23

Give a wooden base to each child. Then, allow him to select five or six other scraps, telling him to sand them all.

Show how glue can be applied with a brush and/or by dipping the wood into the glue container. (Figure 1-23.)

Discuss how a brush that has been used with white glue MUST be kept wet with water, MUST be cleaned thoroughly with soap and water when finished with the project, and MUST be soaked in water for a period of an hour to be certain all glue has been removed. IT THIS IS NOT DONE, THE BRUSH MAY BE RUINED. If glue is still held by the bristles, they become hard and stuck together.

White glue, of course, does the same thing to the wood. When it dries, the glue will be hard, clear and the wooden pieces will be securely joined. Glue the pieces of wood together but make certain each is balanced so that it will not fall off. Stress the fact that a heavy piece cannot be glued on top of a tall, thin piece. It will not stay in place because the weight will make it topple and/or the glue will not dry fast enough to hold it in place. (Figure 1-24.) Gravity plays a very important role in these wooden constructions and kindergarten children soon discover nature's laws. It's upsetting to have a sculpture disintegrate, but with the disintegration comes knowledge. Little children soon learn to solve their problems if given some guidance, and adequate time and freedom to work in their own way. Continually stress: as each piece is added, it should be securely placed. The whole structure should be strong and solid when the glue has dried.

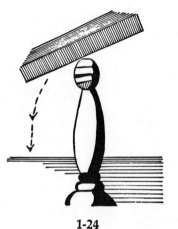

1-24

Other wooden objects, such as popsicle sticks, spools, broom handle sections and matches may be added to create interest. The sculpture may even become something: a sailboat, building, animal, face or even the Washington Monument. (Figure 1-25.)

1-25

The constructions should dry for a full day, after which they may be finished by painting with tempera paint or spray paint. However, there are children who like the wood look and who will not want to paint them.

Specific Skills and Concepts To Be Learned:

1. Wood has a grain and splinters.
2. Two or more pieces of wood can be joined with white glue.
3. White glue requires time to dry, and dries clear and hard.
4. Brushes used in white glue must be cleaned in a different way from brushes used in paint.
5. Making a piece of wooden sculpture involves the ability to balance the various parts.

Adaptations:

This lesson may be adapted for older children by adding more materials and tools. They may wish to work with a partner or a group to make larger and more complicated constructions, and will be interested in working for a much longer period of time.

Another effective way for the older child to work is to have him serve as an aide helping the smaller child to work with wood and glue.

LESSON 7: GET THE ARMS INTO THE ACT! CHALK A RHYTHMIC FREE-ARM MOVEMENT PICTURE

With chalk one can respond in an uninhibited way. Young children create startlingly beautiful designs and pictures in a very few minutes with chalk. Just turn on their imaginations and let their arms swing into action.

Tools, Materials and Equipment:

Large poster chalk	Newspaper
Manila paper	Newsprint

Containers   Newspaper, 12" x 18"
Record Player   Records

Preparation:

Cover table and children. Place chalk in large containers with one container for four children. Disposable aluminum pie or cake tins are fine.

Put a lively record on the record player.

Give each child several 12" x 18" sheets of NEWSPAPER. This is fine to practice on. It is free, can be used for practice purposes, and then thrown away.

Developmental Procedure for Activity:

Begin the lesson with a few preliminary designs on the chalkboard, having the children use chalk on the end or the side. (Figure 1-26.)

Introduce the class to some motion exercises also at the chalkboard.

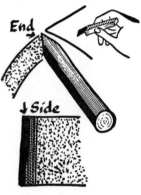

1-26

1. Have children stand and make large circles, swinging their arms, and, at the same time, have them draw circles with chalk on the board. Let arms relax. (Figure 1-27.)

2. Make big, sweeping lines back and forth on the board. Arms must be loose. Draw as long a line as possible, (Figure 1-28.) without moving one's feet or one's position. Relax arms.

3. Draw big, continuous ovals or coils, keeping wrists loose and free. (Figure 1-29.)

1-27

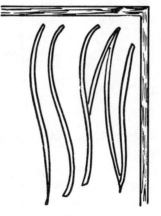

1-28

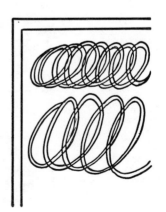

1-29

All these chalk exercises should be done (a) large, (b) loosely, and (c) enjoying the freedom of movement within one's arms.

Next do these same exercises, on a slightly smaller scale, using the 12″ x 18″ newspaper. Add the following to the arm movements.

1. Draw long lines from top to bottom of paper.
2. Make long, curved lines.
3. Try some rhythmical curves and lines, like a series of curved mountains.
4. Draw large, flowing egg shapes.
5. Make some huge flame shapes.

Fill all the space on the paper, being aware of the edges of the paper. Change colors whenever desired. Take a new sheet of paper when all the space has been used up.

Try the same idea using manila or newsprint paper. After several have been made, look at them. Can you see a shape that resembles a flower, a bird, a leaf or anything real? Is it possible to make a picture from it? If so, fill in spaces, add lines, more color, and let the imagination skills take over. (Figure 1-30.)

1-30

1-31

As children work, point out that chalk dust is never blown off the paper for it gets into eyes, and can affect breathing. Pick up the paper, turn it on its side, and dust will slide off onto table top, but NEVER onto the floor.

After designs are completed, fold all the work of a child within a large sheet of newspaper. (Figure 1-31.) Put his name on top, after which he can carry it home without his clothing becoming smeared with dust.

Chalk art can be fixed in various ways, to reduce smearing, but since kindergarten youngsters turn out so many pictures, it's really not practical to do so. If, however, there are special ones, they may be sprayed with hair spray or a commercial fixative. Another method for preventing smearing is to put wax paper over the chalk drawing and press with a warm iron.

Specific Skills and Concepts to Be Learned:

1. Chalk becomes dust and smears.
2. Designs should cover all the paper, out to the edges.
3. Chalk can be used on sides as well as ends.
4. Imagination helps create original drawings.

Adaptations:

This lesson is easily adaptable to the making of posters and murals, whether on paper or chalkboard. For example, flame strokes may become a part of an illustration or poster on fire prevention. (Figure 1-32.)

1-32

LESSON 8: CLAY IS A FAVORITE!
CLAY PRINT PATTERN STAMPING BLOCKS

Impress a design on a block of clay and use it as a stamping block to make simple repeated patterns.

Tools, Materials and Equipment:

Plasticene clay	Newsprint and/or
Tempera paint	construction paper,
Water containers	12" x 18"
Soap	Brushes
	Newspapers

Preparation:

Plasticene clay, an excellent modelling medium for three-dimensional expression, is completely reusable because of its oil base. Since it remains pliable, it can be used over and over again. It's clean in that it is not compatible with water and never dissolves into mud as does ceramic clay.

Plasticene is softened by heat, and hardens with a lowering of the temperature. For that reason, soften the clay slightly by placing it in a sunny spot, or near a heater (but not on a heater for plasticene melts). Children's hands will soften it also.

Developmental Procedure For Activity:

Give children small balls of clay. Suggest they feel, press and roll it in their hands and on the table. Enjoy the clay! Squeeze it! Imagine you're baking bread and knead it. Twist it into a screw shape. Roll back into a ball and make it into a block or a cube shape, with very smooth sides. Use your fingers to smooth and sharpen the corners of the block.

Using only the fingertips, press a design into each side of the block. (Figure 1-33.) This makes a stamping block or STAMPER.

Print with the stamper using the following procedure.

1. Dip brush in water and rub the bristles on a bar of soap. Dip brush into paint and paint one side of stamper. Then press on the paper. (Figure 1-34.) The soap helps the paint to stick to the oily surface of the plasticene. One bar, in a container, is sufficient for four children to work with.

2. Repaint the stamper and press on paper again. Do this until the paper is filled with the printed patterns. (Figure 1-35.)

1-33

1-34

1-35

3. Use the designs made on the other sides of the stamper for more printing fun.

4. Wash the block off with soap and water, dry well with a towel, and make a new stamper.

Specific Skills and Concepts To Be Learned:

1. Plasticene clay becomes soft when warmed up. Water is *not* used to soften it.
2. Plasticene can be used over and over again.
3. It can be molded with the fingers.
4. Tempera paint does not adhere well to the surface of plasticene clay. The addition of soap or detergent alleviates this problem.

Adaptations:

Older children may use the stampers to create various kinds of repetitive printing to make wallpaper and textile patterns. They may also make different stampers by:

1. Rolling clay into a pyramid or cylinder shape instead of cubes.

2. Using forks, buttons, sticks and even nails to impress a design.

These stampers may also be used to stamp designs on flower pots, book covers, T shirts and other practical items. The type of paint, however, will vary according to the item. For example, printing on cloth will require textile paint or acrylics.

LESSON 9: ROLL A COIL!
SIMPLE CLAY COILING EXPERIENCES

Here's a new way to use an old and familiar material. Plasticene clay becomes wall sculpture!

Tools, Materials and Equipment:

Plasticene clay	Bulletin board
Construction paper	Straight pins

Preparation:

The young child is given an opportunity to work with his hands as he manipulates clay. He uses both arm and hand muscles in much the same way as he delightedly makes mud pies or works in the sand at the beach. He enjoys the rolling of clay into long snakes. In this lesson, a tremendous number of snakes or coils will be needed. These will be joined with those made by the entire class to create an assemblage of clay coils.

To begin, warm the clay as prescribed in the previous lesson.

Cover the bulletin board with brightly colored construction paper to serve as a background for the coil assemblage.

Developmental Procedure For Activity:

Give each child several lumps of clay. Roll the clay between hands or on the table to make coils. (Figure 1-36.) Make a lot of them. Make them in different sizes and types. Some may be small; some large. We can make sharp coils and rounded ones; curved and straight; thin and thick; with surfaces which are textured or kept smooth.

1-36

What can we make with coils? Think about it! What objects do you see every day that could be made with one or more coils (ropes, bracelets, rings, worms, snakes, nests, nails, plant stems, pipes, wires, screws)? Make some of these. Bend the coils into circles and ovals. Overlap them. Flatten the ends. Try twisting two coils together or even three. Can you braid some coils?

When coil objects have been completed, talk about the fact that plasticene clay is used over and over and how children, therefore, do not bring these objects home. (They won't like it, but then tell them how their art work will become a part of a classroom project on the bulletin board.) How will the objects be arranged? Who will put up the first piece? (By now, they will have forgotten how upset they were because they couldn't take their work home.) Have a child attach his coil to the bulletin board by using straight pins, stuck right into the clay. Straight pins are used because they can easily be removed, and clay and pins can be reused. Many pins will be needed since the clay is heavy and will fall off if not attached to the wall securely.

Pin up more pieces. How can we place these? Can we join one to another? How? (Press together and use more pins.) All clay objects should be so attached that the finished product will be a gigantic clay design. (Figure 1-37.)

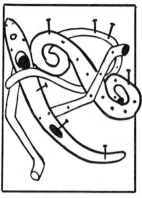

1-37

Continue until all the children's work has been attached. Constantly discuss why it looks good if we put a thin rope with a thick rope or if we go over a coil and under another. Let the children use their own ideas on creating the design. Try to keep it well balanced, so that all the clay is not on one side, with nothing on the other. Also, never completely cover up a child's work. When finished, each child should be able to see the part he contributed.

Specific Skills and Concepts To Be Learned:

1. Plasticene clay is reusable.
2. Clay can be made into coils of various sizes and shapes.
3. Clay sculpture can be used as a wall decoration.
4. Designs should be balanced.
5. Working together can be enjoyable.

Adaptations:

Children of all ages will be fascinated with this clay coil assemblage. Older children can use this same procedure with ceramic clay, omitting the bulletin board assembling. Instead, put the piece together on a wooden board, and have it fired in a kiln. Glaze it, refire and display it as a permanent part of the school's art collection.

LESSON 10: GRAPHICS WITH LITTLE BODIES! HUGE ROLL-OVER BODY PRINTS

In this lesson, little bodies become the tools which create wall paintings and little people become involved in painting without brushes. It's like magic to see the huge double image paintings emerge.

Tools, Materials and Equipment:

Mural paper (Any colors)	Tempera paint
Squeeze bottles	Construction paper
Newspapers	Small jars of tempera paint

Preparation:

Prepare the paint by pouring into squeeze bottles. For an effective painting, always use contrasting color schemes, i.e., some light and dark, some bright and dull colors. Black, orange, green and yellow, for example, are harmonious, pleasant to look at, and excellent for an autumn wall painting.

Check to see that the paint is thick, but not so thick that it will clog the squeeze bottle dispenser. If it is too thick, add a little water and mix well but keep it from becoming thin and watery.

Developmental Procedure For Activity:

Show one or two of Jackson Pollock's paintings, using the drip technique. Explain to the children that there are many different ways to apply paint to a background. Sometimes we use brushes. Sometimes we employ a palette knife. Then we use our fingers or hands as in finger painting, while Jackson Pollock used a dripping technique.

Have a few small jars of paint available in contrasting colors. Drip the paint here and there all over a piece of construction paper, trying to establish a pleasing design—not all dark on one side and all light on the other, not all the paint in one corner and nothing on the rest of the page. Let it please the eye!

Now introduce the idea of doing a drip painting using one's body. Clear a large space in the room and cover the floor with newspapers. A large sheet of mural paper (about 6' - 8' long) is placed over the newspaper. Make certain that the newspaper covers a much larger area of space than the mural paper (to keep floor clean).

Using the squeeze bottles, demonstrate how to drip the paint by walking on or around the paper. Drip in curves, straight lines, zigzags, thick and thin lines, etc. Let one child at a time drip the various colors. (Figure 1-38.) All children should eventually have several turns, but maintain CONTROL over the situation. Quite a bit of paint is dripped on but this is done quickly before it has a chance to dry.

Place two sheets of mural paper (same size as the first) directly on top of the painted paper. One is for the paint to be transferred onto and the second is to guarantee that children's clothes will not get painted as they become actively involved in spreading the paint.

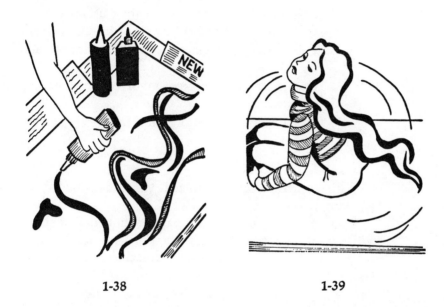

1-38   1-39

Line the children up and have them walk slowly over the top of the mural papers. Then let them do various activities on top of the paper, beginning with one child performing at a time. Use their bodies to roll over from one end of the paper to the other. Sit on it and wiggle across the paper. Hop all the way across on one foot. Slide feet as if skating on ice. Invent other physical activities that can be done for a short time before the paint gets too dry. (Figure 1-39.) Explain that an artist's body, as well as his intelligence, should become involved with his painting.

In about ten minutes, stop all activity, and remove two top sheets, showing children how they have made identical paintings. Find a BIG storage space, such as a quiet hall or an unused classroom and let dry thoroughly. A class can usually do two sets of identical paintings in a fifty minute period.

After drying, the paintings can be hung in the hall or in the classroom for all to enjoy. Other alternatives would be (a) to cut them in pieces for children to take home, or (b) if it is the holiday season, use them for gift wrapping paper.

Specific Skills and Concepts To Be Learned:

1. There are many ways to apply paint to a background.
2. Paintings look better when they utilize contrasting colors (dark and light . . . . . or bright and dull).
3. Paint can be transferred from one surface to another by rubbing.
4. Bodies should become involved in painting experiences.
5. Jackson Pollock was an important American artist.

Adaptations:

This approach can be utilized with older children in the following ways:

1. Glue black construction paper silhouettes of sports activities on top of the drip paintings. (Figure 1-40.)
2. Use these paintings for a quick scenery background for a class play.

1-40

Teaching Through Sensory Experiences

PART TWO: TEACHING THROUGH SENSORY EXPERIENCES

We gain knowledge and understanding of our environment through the use of our senses. Every object has a visual and tactile quality. Each has a specific odor. Some make special sounds. Each has a distinctive flavor or taste. A child's survival depends upon his ability to recognize, classify and utilize these special qualities in a safe and effective way.

Sensory awareness is vital and basic to a child's growth and development. He takes in information as his senses examine each new object and situation in his life. He becomes receptive to his own feelings and sees new relationships. He learns to be selective and discriminating. For these reasons, every elementary school should include EDUCATION FOR THE SENSES in its curriculum.

Part Two of this book has been planned to increase sensory perception. In each of the next four chapters, the child will be led through activities that are designed to motivate by means of firsthand and vicarious experiences. The child will be guided to investigate an object by looking, listening, smelling, tasting, touching and manipulating, whether that object is a lump of clay, or a soft, furry kitten. He will bring into action a personalized view of that object when he stores it in his memory bank or when he uses it in his art expressions. This view, of course, will be multi-sensory.

NOTE: From this section on, the lessons will be basically for the primary grades 1, 2, and 3, rather than for the kindergarten child, since his curriculum should be more exploratory as shown in Chapter One. After his involvement in the developmental experiences, and as he becomes capable of performing more advanced activities, the very young child can continue with Chapter Two.

PART

2

2

Touching Is Permissible:

Developing the Tactile Sense

Tactile organs are distributed throughout the skin all over the body. The sense of touch or feeling consists of the response of the body to a physical stimulus such as: pain, pressure, heat and cold. Pain receptors are the deepest within the skin while the other receptors lie in the outer layers. Tactile sensations result from the stimulation of a combination of these receptors.

The young child goes through a natural phase in his development where he wants to touch. This, therefore, becomes an important part of his art experiences. Touching is a way of learning and, too often, we restrict by saying "DON'T TOUCH." This procedure is reversed in these lessons wherein we say "PLEASE TOUCH." From the touching of art media and objects, to the touching of one's own art products, discoveries are made about the qualities of being soft or hard, smooth or rough, wet, dry or slippery.

LESSON 1: TEXTURE IT ROUGH!
COVER OBJECTS WITH SAND AND GRAVEL

Paint with glue, sprinkle on sand, and feel! It's rough!

Tools, Materials and Equipment:

Colored and/or natural sand or gravel	Tempera paint
	Containers for sand
Heavy cardboard	Scissors for cutting yarn

White glue	Cotton
Rubber bands	Newspapers
Yarn	Jars
Brushes	Cloth for blindfolds

Preparation:

Purchase colored sand (gravel) . . . . . or make your own. To make colored sand, use tempera paint. Half fill a jar with sand, add one teaspoon of dry powdered paint, put top on jar and shake. If the color is not bright enough, add more paint.

Colored gravel can be made in the same way, but use thick, moist tempera in place of powdered paint. After mixing, spread out the gravel onto newspaper, giving it plenty of time to dry, and move it around every hour so that it does not become one big gravel lump.

It is well to have an assortment of several colors and natural (or beige) but NO BLACK, for black blurs the design.

Developmental Procedure for Activity:

To begin this lesson, blindfold the children. Have them put cotton in their ears, (Parents and older children can help in this.) Place very textural materials on a table. Use shells, bricks, stones, fabrics, and anything that has a distinctive feeling. Place a few pieces of sandpaper of varying degrees of coarseness among the items.

Have children attempt to identify an object in their minds solely by feeling it. Concentrate on how it feels. What is this object that I'm touching?

Remove objects. Take off blindfolds. Discuss what each felt like. Try to name the objects before bringing them back to show the class.

Now arrange rubber bands, or pieces of yarn, on heavy cardboard to form a design. Glue firmly in place and let dry. These outlines give a structure with which to work and ties the design together. (Figure 2-1.)

Paint the area inside each space with glue and sprinkle on sand or gravel, working with one color at a time. Sprinkle on and shake off excess back into the correct color container.

(Figure 2-2.) Continue until all areas and the background have been filled in.

2-1

2-2

Try sand and gravel together for variations in texture. Note the difference in the tactile quality. Use small pebbles, stones, or shells for accents or for eyes, inside of ears, and noses. Drop on some extra glue to keep these firm.

Specific Skills and Concepts To Be Learned:

1. Sand and gravel can be colored or left their natural colors.
2. Both can be glued to cardboard or other surfaces.
3. Sand and gravel feel rough and gritty.

Adaptations:

Use the techniques described in this lesson with various colors of glitter, combine with bits of colored yarn, or try coloring sugar or salt with food coloring. Try kosher salt, too; it's more coarse. Do they work as well as sand and gravel?

LESSON 2: PAINT WITH SOFTNESS!
COTTON AND TISSUE PAINTING

Using a light touch with a cotton ball, children can paint a soft background for a tissue paper still life.

Tools, Materials and Equipment:

Cotton balls	White glue
Tissue paper	Tempera paint
Newspaper	Paint containers
Manila paper 12" x 16"	Scissors
Paper towels	

Preparation:

Have the children arrange a still life using ceramics, bottles, toys, or flowers on a small table or desk that has been covered with smooth textured fabric, preferably in one color (blue, or green, but NOT blue and green). Arrange in front of a plain section of the wall.

A still life can be moved around and adjusted until it pleases the eye. Once the arrangement is set up, it can be allowed to remain in that position for as long as desired, thus giving the students plenty of time for a thorough study.

Developmental Procedure For Activity:

What does the term STILL LIFE mean? It refers to an arrangement of inanimate objects, such as fruit, bread, books, as well as those items listed above. Suggest that children walk around the still life, observing it from all angles. Does it look the same from all sides? Why does it change? Which view is the best? Which would be harder to draw or paint? What if you were looking at it from the ceiling? . . . . . or if you were seated on the floor?

Compose a still life by cutting the shapes out of tissue. Place and arrange them on manila paper. Are they too small? Then make larger ones. Are they too big? Use only a part of them, and imagine the rest of the shape as being off the paper. (Figure 2-3.)

2-3

Does our still life need something else? Of course, a background or wall, and the cloth on the table is missing too! For these, two colors of tempera paint in flat containers are needed. Use a cotton ball, instead of a brush, to apply the paint. Dip it into the paint and press lightly on a paper towel to remove excess. Blot it on the paper. (Figure 2-4.) (As a rule, several blots may be made before redipping into the paint. This gives a textured, dark-light effect.)

2-4

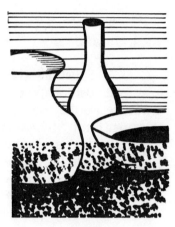

2-5

Continue this blob painting all over the paper, trying to show a difference between the wall and the table. This can be done by applying more paint to the place where the table begins as opposed to the end of the wall, or by changing colors. Be sure to use a new piece of cotton when switching to a new color.

Allow paint to dry thoroughly and then carefully glue the tissue paper still life in place. Notice how the paint underneath the tissue shows through, creating a partially transparent effect. (Figure 2-5.)

Specific Skills and Concepts To Be Learned:

1. A still life is an arrangement of inanimate objects.
2. A ball of cotton feels soft and creates a soft, mottled effect when used in place of a brush, for applying paint.

3. What one sees when looking at a still life arrangement depends upon where one is sitting or standing in the room.
4. Partial shapes can be used in a still life, letting the viewer's eyes imagine the rest of the shapes being off the paper.
5. Tissue paper can be combined with paint to achieve a partially transparent effect.

Adaptations:

1. Substitute construction paper for tissue.
2. Before applying the paint, wet the surface of the paper. Then use the cotton ball dipped in paint and pull across the paper for a different effect.
3. Try a piece of colored construction paper for the background instead of manila.
4. Apply paint with cotton swabs instead of balls. These can be rinsed off, before using a new color.
5. Study the still life paintings of great artists such as: Paul Cezanne, Auguste Renoir, Vincent Van Gogh, Jan Vermeer, Pablo Picasso and Claude Monet.

LESSON 3: SMOOTH IT WITH WAX! CRAYON TRANSFERRED DESIGNS

Did you know that crayons can be melted and transferred from one paper to another?

Tools, Materials and Equipment:

Wax crayons	Iron
Vellum paper	Newspapers
Plywood (large piece)	Books with good illustrations (drawings or paintings, not photographs)

Preparation:

Make your own ironing board by covering a large piece of plywood with a pad of newspapers.

Developmental Procedure for Activity:

Ask the children to draw a crayon picture of a recent experience. Did they see a musical? an accident? a fire? Did they go fishing, swimming or to a ball game? Draw something remembered from the excitement! . . . . . but only a small part.

(If ideas lag, lead the children to talk about their recent experiences . . . . . or let them make one up and then illustrate it.)

Discuss how artists are employed to illustrate books. Show several examples of book illustrations, pointing out that each picture is only a fragment of the experiences described within the book. Have children look at their own drawings. Are they fragments of an experience or have they tried to tell the whole experience? Draw another . . . . . but ONLY A VERY SMALL PART OF THE SPECIAL EVENT.

Begin with strong crayoned outlines, stressing that students work LARGE. If they draw people, make them BIG. Animals should be BIG. Flowers should be BIG. Point out that large objects actually will mean fewer objects in the picture. Make your drawing a close-up of something, like a close-up view of the sun, or part of the sun. (Figure 2-6.)

Fill in each space of the entire piece of paper with brightly colored crayon, pressing hard, and coloring heavily for that extra brightness, leaving no empty white spaces. Feel the smoothness of the wax crayon.

Fill in the background, too. (Figure 2-7.) If this bothers the child, and he cannot fill in the background smoothly, have him separate it into sectional patterns. (Figure 2-8.)

2-6

2-7

2-8

2-9

After the design has been completed, place it on the ironing board with the crayon side down, on top of another piece of drawing paper.

Press with a hot iron, melting the wax and making it permeate the top paper. Some of the crayon will be transferred onto the bottom paper, resulting in two designs. (Figure 2-9.)

Specific Skills and Concepts To Be Learned:

1. Wax crayons can be melted.
2. Illustrations show part of an experience.
3. Illustrating can become one's life work, a vocation.
4. Wax designs can be transferred from one paper to another by the use of a hot iron.

Adaptations:

1. Try dripping candlewax on paper and note the difference from the wax of colored crayons. Do they feel different?

2. Dissolve crayons by dipping in turpentine and rub on paper. Does the crayon feel the same as when it was used in the dry state? Has the waxy quality disappeared?

LESSON 4: CONVERT SOFT POWDER TO HARD OBJECT! PLASTER DROPLETS ON WOOD

Look to nature for the nucleus of an interesting art activity.

Tools, Materials and Equipment:

Plaster	Construction paper
Rocks	Brushes
Plaster Containers	Tempera paint
Felt pens	White glue
Sandpaper	Newspaper
Scissors	

Preparation:

Collect rocks or large pebbles and clean by washing in soap and water.

Prepare the children for plaster work by discussing the following essentials:

1. Plaster will clog the sink. DON'T LET IT GO DOWN THE DRAIN.

2. Wash hands in a basin of water and dump outdoors. (It won't hurt the grass.)

3. Always use THROW-AWAY containers when mixing plaster. (Saves work and clogged drains.)

4. Keep wet and dry plaster off the floor, or footprints will be everywhere throughout the school . . . . . in the lavatory, at the drinking fountain, at the main office . . . . . and then such unhappy faces will appear on custodians and administrators.

Developmental Procedure For Activity:

Look at rocks and pebbles. How do they feel? Roll them over in your hand. Rub your finger over the surface. Feel the shape. Is the surface completely free from any irregularities, roughness, or projections? These feeling experiences are essential in developing one's ability to see. Without touching different surfaces, we could not reconstruct certain experiences in our mind's eye. (Figure 2-10.)

2-10

Now turn on your imagination! What real objects do these rocks and pebbles suggest? Heads? Bugs? Animals? Sculptures? Faces? Talk about it, and then transfer this learning to working with plaster.

Cover the table with newspaper and mix plaster. Use as follows:

1. Pour in two parts of plaster to one part of water and mix until all the powder has been absorbed. (Let the children feel and compare the soft quality of the plaster when in powder form with the pliable quality of the plaster after it has been combined with the water.

2. Pour out blobs onto the newspaper. These should look somewhat like rocks or large pebbles. (Figure 2-11.)

2-11

2-12

3. Mix another batch, letting it harden slightly. Give each child a small amount with which to work but stress that the plaster will begin to set in a very short time and will no longer be plastic or pliable. Children, therefore, must work quickly to form a plaster rock by pushing it around with their fingers. (Figure 2-12.)

4. When dry, plaster changes into a hard substance. It will set in about an hour. As it sets, let the children feel the heat that comes about because of the chemical reaction taking place. For a day or so, the edges of the plaster forms will be especially breakable, so treat them carefully.

After the plaster rocks are thoroughly dried, look at them. Recall the discussions on the natural rocks and pebbles. What do our rocks resemble? Turn them over. Smooth them with sandpaper if desired. Scrape off some of the plaster with an old knife, but BE CAREFUL. Use a few strokes of a felt pen to make a face! Draw a bug's head on one end and paint the rest in appropriate colors! Make something from the plaster rock: a head, bug, mask, animal, ... a very interesting creature. The children can go as far as their imaginations will take them.

2-13

Bits of plaster or construction paper can be glued on for ears, hats, legs, accents, or as desired. These make very nice paperweights that can be used as gifts. (Figure 2-13.)

Specific Skills and Concepts To Be Learned:

1. Plaster changes from soft, to warm, to hard.
2. Rocks and pebbles have interesting forms.
3. Plaster blobs can also have interesting forms.
4. Plaster is a material that demands careful use so that it doesn't clog sink drains and doesn't mess up the school.

Adaptations:

1. Use rocks instead of plaster for paperweights.
2. Make rock shapes with papier-maché over stuffed paper bags. These can be turned into the objects they resemble.

LESSON 5: FABRICS ARE DIFFERENT! MAKING A FEELING CREATURE

Help your students learn how to design an imaginary FEEL-ING creature using textural cloth.

Tools, Materials and Equipment:

Scissors	Textural cloth
White glue	Containers for fabrics
Oaktag, large	

Preparation:

Collect textural fabrics such as: corduroy, burlap, velour, felt, terry cloth, tweed, satin, netting and velvet. Cut the fabric into small squares about 2″ x 2″. Place these in containers, one container for each fabric to make it simple for the children to select what they want to use.

Developmental Procedure for Activity:

Feeling, as stated in previous lessons, is an important part of the art experience. Art education develops feeling as an in-

2-14

2-15

strument for expression. By touching, we learn about texture or the surface quality of an object. Eventually, we develop the ability to feel with our eyes.

An excellent feeling experience is to have the child work with fabrics. Have him finger them, rub his hand over them and at the same time, move his eyes over their surfaces. These sensory impressions help him to create a conceptual image of the texture and the object itself, and are essential to the child's thinking, feeling, and expressions.

Now draw an outline on oaktag of a FEELING CREATURE. He can be utterly imaginative or realistic: a gingerbread boy, a creature living underwater, or on another planet. Cut the shape out. (Figure 2-14.)

Glue textural scraps all over the creature. Use as many different textures as is desired. Make the creature exciting to feel by having many different textures, some rough, some soft, smooth, slippery, etc. (Figure 2-15.)

Specific Skills and Concepts To Be Learned:

1. Texture is the surface quality of an object.
2. Fabrics have many different kinds of textures.
3. Touching fabrics, and looking at them at the same time, makes one understand more about the fabrics themselves.

Adaptations:

Design a feeling creature with two pieces of textural cloth, sew around edges, on wrong side of cloth, turn inside out, and stuff with old stockings. Add accents by gluing on other textural fabrics for eyes, buttons, clothing, etc. These can be used as a pillow if made large enough.

Children can also gain a great deal of cutting experience, if they are allowed to cut their own textural squares. However, they must have:

1. Adequate time.
2. Sharp scissors.

LESSON 6: FEEL A SHELL!
CREATING SHELL DESIGNS

Shells are a fascinating way to study design in nature.

Tools, Materials and Equipment:

Newspapers	Small brush
White glue	Pipe cleaners
Wood scraps	Driftwood
Shells	

Preparation:

Collect seashells of all kinds and sizes and clean them with soap and water, scrubbing with a small brush. Let dry thoroughly. DO NOT COLLECT SHELLS WITH THE LIVING ANIMALS IN THEM. Nature has created them for a specific purpose and children should be taught not to interfere with, but to respect all living creatures as a part of the balance of Nature.

Conduct research on shells:

1. What are their names and origins?

2. Learn all about them! Collecting shells was an ancient pursuit. They were used in art and religion, as decorative objects, and even as money.

3. Learn to look at shells to see the beauty of their design, color and shape. Note how the designs and forms are repeated. Look to see what the ocean and storms have done to them. Are they broken, chipped, or discolored?

4. Learn about the animals who formerly used the shells as their homes.

Developmental Procedure for Activity:

After studying about shells, invite the children to use them in an art experience. Discuss how shells can be used to make miniature sculptures by gluing them together, even using fragments of surf-tossed shells. They can be pieced together to make tiny birds or animals. Add a pipe cleaner or a button to make small accents. (Figure 2-16.)

2-16

For a very tactile experience, use small shells or pieces of

shells to create a decorative collage on a piece of driftwood. (Figure 2-18.) . . . . . Or make a collage with a scrap wooden background.

Sandpaper the wood first, smoothing all sides and edges. Then glue the shells onto the background in a design. These small shells may be clustered to make larger units for a more consolidated composition. For example:

1. Make a border around the edge of the wood with similar kinds of shells. (Figure 2-18.)

2. Plan a composition using simple basic shapes in the center and determine what kinds of shells will be used. Emphasize the need for bold, simple shapes and color contrasts between the shapes. For example, create a pattern in the center with rays coming outward toward the edge with other shells. (Figure 2-19.)

2-17

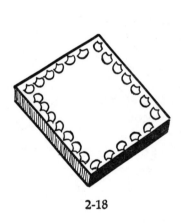

2-18

2-19

3. Carefully glue each shell by painting the underside with plenty of white glue, which will be clear when dry.

4. Let the color of the wooden background show between the pieces. (This can be varnished or shellacked when the shells have been glued and the glue has thoroughly dried.)

Craftsmanship is extremely important when using shells. Care must be taken in cleaning, designing and gluing.

Specific Skills and Concepts To Be Learned:

1. Shells are one of nature's most exquisite examples of design.
2. Well-designed objects are created to serve a function and to be beautiful as well. Shells are an excellent example of this form following function. The animal's home was made to fit him exactly, to suit Nature's purposes, and at the same time, the shell is beautiful.
3. Shells can be used to create art forms such as miniature sculptures and shell collages.

Adaptations:

There are many ways in which shells can be utilized in art experiences, such as the following:

1. Make jewelry (pins, earrings, necklaces and bracelets). This is an activity more suited to upper grades since the skills are too involved for young children. For example, they would have difficulty with the drilling of holes in shells.

2. The careful, precise drawing of all different kinds of shells, using artists' pens and India ink, is fine practice for the artistically gifted. Such an experience involves the child in looking, analyzing and interpreting design.

LESSON 7: WORKING WET AND SLIPPERY! PAPIER-MACHE FULL BALLOON MASKS

The strip method of papier-maché can be used for forming objects over a base of clay, paper or even a balloon, as shown in this lesson.

Tools, Materials and Equipment:

Round balloons	Wallpaper paste
Paste Containers	Newspaper
Tempera paint	Brushes
Vaseline	String
Cardboard	Masking tape

Preparation:

2-20

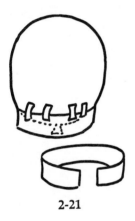

2-21

1. Blow up balloons, knotting tightly with string, so that no air escapes or the mask will collapse. If the mask is to be worn, the balloon must be larger than the child's head.

2. Attach a name tag to string at the base of the balloon. (Figure 2-20.)

3. Cut a strip of cardboard 2" wide and long enough to slip over the child's head. Fasten together securely with masking tape.

4. Place the blown-up balloon on top of the cardboard cylinder with the tied end down. Tape balloon to cardboard. (Figure 2-21.)

5. Cover the balloon with a thin layer of vaseline.

6. Mix wallpaper paste according to the manufacturer's instructions, getting all the lumps out. Fill cut-down bleach bottles one-half full of paste.

7. Tear newspaper into 1" x 6" strips. (Tear with the printed columns.) Place black and white, and colored comic strips in separate containers. Tear paper towels into strips and put in another container. These are used for separate layers of pasted paper as will be explained later in this chapter.

8. Spread newspapers over working areas and all places where masks will be stored as they dry. PLENTY OF SPACE WILL BE REQUIRED.

Developmental Procedure for Activity:

Begin by dipping strips of newspaper into paste. Place between two fingers (Figure 2-22.), and draw off excess paste letting it drip back into the container.

2-22

Carefully place strip on balloon. STRESS that children FEEL the paste, FEEL the smoothness, or the lumps if the paste has not been mixed adequately. Smell the paste, too, and note its unique odor. FEEL the smoothness as each strip of paper is applied to the balloon.

Dip another newspaper strip in paste and place partly on top of previous piece. Continue to cover the balloon and cardboard cylinder with overlapped strips placing some across one way, some the other, until every space is covered. (The overlapping is essential for strength.)

2-23

Now use the colored comic strips and cover with a second layer, then a third layer of black and white newspaper, a fourth of colored, and a fifth of paper towel strips as the final coat. Cover the entire surface with a coat of the paste for additional strength when dry. (Figure 2-23.)

Allow to dry thoroughly for several days. When *thoroughly* dry, use a pin to puncture the balloon. Listen to the sounds as the balloon pulls away from the papier-maché walls. (This may happen during the drying period, so don't be surprised if it sounds as if there are strange creatures inhabiting the classroom, making crackling sounds.) (Figure 2-24.)

If the mask is to be worn, cut holes for eyes and nose. Add any extra features by gluing on felt or construction paper ears, eyebrows, mouth, tongue; yarn hair. Paint with tempera paint. (Figure 2-25.)

2-24

2-25

Specific Skills and Concepts To Be Learned:

1. Masks can be made to fit over one's entire head by using papier-maché over a balloon.
2. Wallpaper paste is slippery when wet.
3. Layers of pasted paper become extremely hard and durable when dry.
4. Rubber balloons shrink inside a papier-maché shell as the water and paste dry out.

Adaptations:

Older children can add cardboard noses, ears, etc. and attach firmly with masking tape to the blown-up balloon, before the papier-maché is applied. The features are also covered with papier-maché.

For a variation, use the balloon to make head people, omitting the cardboard cylinder base (for neck) and covering the entire balloon. (Figure 2-26.) The arms and legs are made with construction paper. For this round fellow, three solid coats of paper and paste would be sufficient. The mask requires more layers for strength since it will be worn by the child.

2-26

3

Sound Off on Art:

Developing the Auditory Sense

Sound is a sensory experience that all children with normal hearing capacity can receive through their ears, perceive mentally, and describe verbally and artistically. It is caused by the vibrating of an object. It travels through mediums, such as air or water. All sound can be described in terms of length of duration (long-short), pitch (high-low), intensity (loud-soft) and timbre (distinctive tone which gives it its unique quality).

Sound is a form of communication. Children who have a hearing impairment are cut off from the environment in which they live, and are held back, to a great extent, in their learning development. Sounds help us locate objects and tell us what is taking place around us. We hear a puppy scratching at the door and we know where he is, and what he wants. A whistling kettle calls us to the kitchen to shut off the range and stop the whistle. An alarm clock rings to tell us it is time to get up. A horn warns of the approach of a vehicle and its possible danger. The human voice teaches us our language and our culture. Auditory sensitivity, therefore, is of extreme importance to the elementary school child and his or her growth.

In this chapter, the sound awareness of children is encouraged, strengthened and developed by art activities that work with, and relate to, distinctive sounds. Experiences will involve the use of many varieties of sounds: musical, background, recorded, natural, man-made, unwanted sounds; sounds in art; and even the sounds of commercial sound makers.

LESSON 1: CITY SOUNDS VIBRATE!
MAKING POSTERS TO ILLUSTRATE CITY LIFE

City life teems with noise and distinctive sounds. It vibrates with vitality.

Tools, Materials and Equipment:

Manila paper 12" x 18"
Rulers
Pencils
Records, tapes, slides,
  films, as desired

Newsprint paper
Felt-tipped markers
Record player, tape recorder,
  film or slide projector,
  as desired.

Preparation:

Arrange a bulletin board based on city life: its people, recreation, architecture, problems, culture, vocations, and transportation. Discuss the city and become involved in its eccentricites. Read about it. Vicariously live in it! Draw city scenes using pencils and/or crayons. Sketch a lot of these, making each quickly and without undue concentration on good drawing or fine details. Get the feeling, the ideas, and the background sounds down on paper.

What are background sounds? They consist of many different kinds of noises, all blending together into a generalized sound movement. Tape some of the school background sounds (cafeteria, playground and ball games). Introduce city background sounds by (a) a field trip to the city, (b) viewing slides or films, or (c) playing a tape or record of city sounds. These can actually be taped from television or radio, where noises are constant, as we hear engines running, horns beeping, tires and brakes squealing, the subways, airplanes taking off, and a myriad of other city sounds.

Developmental Procedure for Activity:

Make a poster that will show the sounds of the city. Stress the following:

1. A poster is actually a salesperson whose aim is to sell the city to the people who look at it.

2. It uses color to attract people's attention.
3. Good spacing, lettering and originality are emphasized.
4. A good poster must be simple and eye-catching.

Advance planning is essential to save time and improve the quality of the art work. Using newsprint, block in, with pencil, what is going to be shown on the poster. Roughly sketch in the words, or slogan, that will be conveying the message. The lettering must conform to the message. For example, what are noisy words or expressions? SHOUT them out! SCREAM a reply! CLANG an engine! ROAR into the city! (Figure 3-1.) List these on the chalkboard for future reference. If fire engines and firemen are to be used on the poster, the lettering could be enveloped in flames. (Figure 3-2.)

3-1

3-2

3-3

Sound words can be utilized, too, in the slogan. Pitter-patter along the sidewalks. Don't let the crowds CRUSH you! SCRAPED your fender? Traffic SNARL! (Figure 3-3.)

Lettering may be drawn on freely, carefully made with a ruler and pen, or even placed on an angle for added interest. Stress that lettering must be simple, well spaced and readable. *Legibility is of utmost importance*, more so than perfection of lettering.

Select and use color to dramatize the theme, realizing that a few colors usually are more bold and striking than many. Think about colors: what ones are noisy and which are quiet? (Red screams while blue is gentle and shy.)

Think, also, about noisy and quiet lines. A zig-zag makes us think of a thunderbolt or a traffic jam (Figure 3-4), while a horizontal line seems to denote peace and quiet. (Figure 3-5.)

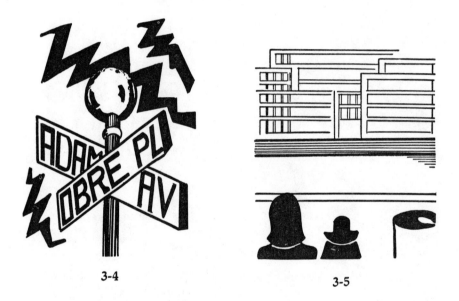

3-4

3-5

Colored backgrounds can be used. A light background with dark lettering is effective as is a dark background with bold, bright lettering. (For the beginning poster-maker, however, it is suggested that manila paper be used.)

Use a symbol to emphasize and enliven the poster. It will not only illustrate the theme, but it can reduce the number of words needed. For these, it may be essential to refer to the quick get-acquainted-with-the-city drawings done at the beginning of this lesson. Another note of caution would be that symbols, also, should avoid excessive details and should be easily identifiable with the subject matter.

When a good design has been evolved, pencil it in on the manila paper and complete it by coloring with crayons or felt-tipped pens.

Specific Skills and Concepts To Be Learned:

1. Background sounds consist of many noises all being made at the same time.
2. They differ according to their specific locale.
3. Posters are made to sell something.
4. Simplicity, good spacing and legibility are the vital organs of a poster.

Adaptations:

Create posters with other themes based on different background sounds (the zoo, circus, fair, concert, sports events, the beach, an accident).

LESSON 2: WATER MAKES SOUNDS AND SO DOES MUSIC! TEMPERA PAINT THE SOUND OF MOVING WATER

There is a distinct relationship between musical sound and artistic expression. See for yourself!

Tools, Materials and Equipment:

Record player	Tempera paint
Projector	Newspaper
Manila paper	Brushes
Water containers	Slides and/or ocean-sea-
Record—Vltava	river-stream photographs
("The Moldau")	or art reproductions
by Smetana	

Preparation:

Introduce the subject of water sounds by showing photographs, reproductions and/or slides of artists' paintings of bodies of water. See the works of Winslow Homer, Emil Nolde,

Gustave Courbet, Oskar Kokoschka, Jacopo Tintoretto, William Turner and any others that have worked with this theme. At the same time, play the record *Vltava ("The Moldau")* quietly in the background.

Then discuss why they are all so different. Stress that artists show their impressions in their own way. Some are realistic. They visualize real looking pictures in their mind's eye. Others express themselves emotionally through abstract or nonobjective designs.

If you are a realistic person, what pictures do you imagine as you listen to the music? (Figure 3-6.) What mood? Happy? Sad? Thoughtful? Remember if you are realistic, you would paint your picture using true coloring as you see it.

3-6

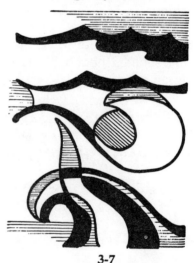

3-7

If you are an emotional artist, what types of lines do you think would portray your feelings about the music? What shapes? What rhythms? (Figure 3-7.) Loud sounds with bright, huge colors and shapes? Soft sounds with pastel, soft colors, lines and shapes? What kinds of lines portray the melody? Sharp? Curved?

Introduce and play the record again, telling children it was composed by Bedrich Smetana. Smetana was from Bohemia, a region in central Europe, on the border of West Germany and Czechoslovakia. The area was a heavily forested mountainous place. The *Moldau* is a symphonic poem in which Smetana tells the story of a river as it journeys from its origin until it reaches the river bed. Listen intently for the distinguishing sounds.

Developmental Procedure for Activity:

Continue to play the *Moldau* throughout this activity. Instruct students to paint what the music says to them. Improvise a picture. What does the music reveal by its sounds? Show them in your painting. What pictures or designs can you see in your mind as you listen to the sounds of the music? What colors portray the mood of the various parts? Are you a realistic or emotional artist? Your picture will show this.

Allow children to make as many paintings as they desire. Some will paint at a faster rate than others. Also, some will be unhappy with their paintings; throw them away, and start over.

Specific Skills and Concepts To Be Learned:

1. The sounds of nature can be interpreted through music and art.
2. Music and painting are both expressive arts.
3. Music can be interpreted with paint. The results, however, are dependent upon the mood of the music and the style of the artist.

Adaptations:

1. Interpret music with finger paint, transferring the rhythms into the painted design.

2. Use only one color of paint. Begin at the top of the paper and record your feelings about the sounds of the music by making lines, dots, curves, going across the page, in and out. As a loud sound occurs, put it down on the paper. When the sound goes from loud to soft, record it with the paint.

LESSON 3: ANIMALS SOUND DIFFERENT! MAKING CLAY SCULPTURES OF ANIMALS

Animal noises are natural sounds, similar to children's speaking, crying, laughing and singing. Utilize these sounds by working three-dimensionally with clay.

Tools, Materials and Equipment:

Ceramic clay	Basin of water
Newspaper	Water containers
Record and record player and/or tapes and tape recorder	Pictures, slides, films of animals, as desired.
Old pen or pencil	Popsicle sticks
Brushes	Tempera paint
	Boxes

Preparation:

The noises animals make often suggest a visual image to the child who has been exposed to, or seen the animals live, on television, or in films. Therefore, begin this activity by becoming acquainted with animals of all kinds, wild and domesticated, young and adult. Look at pictures, view films or slides, visit a zoo or bring in pets. Discuss how they live, feel, sound and even how they smell. Listen to animal sounds on records or tapes. Hear the noises and guess who made them.

Prepare the children for working with clay by stressing:

1. All the clay bits are to be kept on the newspaper-covered table. Never let them fall on the floor or into the sink.

2. When clay work is finished . . . . . Dust your hands together, over the table before going to wash in the basin of water. This is done to keep sink drain from clogging. Finally, wash off hands thoroughly at the sink with soap and water.

3. All completed sculptures should have the children's names on the bottom. Use an old pen or pencil for this.

4. Newspapers that have been used on the tables must be rolled up so that all bits of clay remain securely inside. Then place them in wastebasket.

Demonstrate the necessary routines for working with clay by showing:

1. How to join clay: Weld all parts together. Put a little water on the two pieces to be joined. Scratch both surfaces with your fingernail, roughing it up. (Figure 3-8a). Then use great pressure to push the two pieces together, smoothing the connection with your fingers. (Figure 3-8b.)

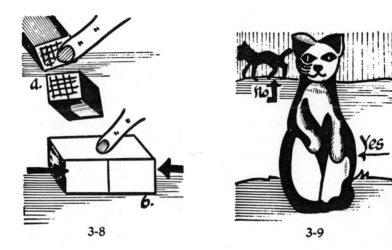

3-8   3-9

2. If the clay gets too dry, dip a finger into water and rub it on the clay. Do this for cracks, too. Remember: TOO MUCH WATER BECOMES MUD.

3. All sculptures should be thick and short, for the thin, long pieces will fall off as they dry. (Figure 3-9.)

4. Whenever you don't like what you have made, squash it, and try again.

Cover the tables and storage places with newspaper, making certain the clay will be allowed to dry slowly in a cool location. Fill water containers one-half full with water. Fill a big basin with water.

Prepare the clay, by cutting it into 4" cubes (at least one per child is needed.)

Developmental Procedure for Activity:

What can we do with clay (pull, push, squeeze, roll, flatten, break, make holes through it, pinch, punch, knead, weld, mold it)? Clay is wonderful to manipulate. If feels good. It's smooth and cool. It has a musty, earthy smell, but do you think we could make something from it? We can't sit here and squeeze if for a whole period. Perhaps we could push and pull some animals out of it.

Play the animal tape or record. With all these animal sounds, are there any that make you feel like making the animal that made one of the noises? Let's make some clay animals from these sounds! The animal can be real or imaginative. For example, a parrot, or any bird for that matter, has feathers, a beak and a tail. We could make a parrot look real with the feathers, beak and tail. On the other hand, if you know a parrot sound, but you're not sure exactly how one looks, and you'd like to make a parrot, make one, but make him look the way you imagine him to be.

Use fingers or a popsicle stick to indent the eyes, feathers or fur. (Figure 3-10.)

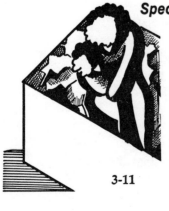

3-10

Be sure to complete the animals in one period, for the clay hardens overnight. (Clay can be worked on over a longer period, if it is kept moist.)

When modelling has been completed, allow the sculptures to dry thoroughly. They then can be fired in a kiln (ceramic oven) or painted with tempera paint. Firing in the kiln hardens the sculpture and makes it less apt to break, but young children have difficulty joining the forms, and sometimes the clay contains air bubbles that will explode when fired. For these reasons, animals should be dried, painted, and carefully sent home in a box surrounded by a cushion of newspaper. (Figure 3-11.)

Specific Skills and Concepts To Be Learned:

1. Sounds and pictures help us to know more about animals, and to recognize them. Seeing real animals makes our knowledge more complete for we can then feel, see, and smell them.

2. Ceramic clay hardens when dry, but is extremely breakable unless fired in a kiln.

3. A kiln is a ceramic oven that fires (bakes) the clay to a very high temperature (around 2000° F.), thus drying out the water and hardening the clay.

3-11

4. Clay routines must be observed faithfully:
   A. Use of water softens clay and smooths out cracks.
   B. Clay is joined or welded together by texturing it, moistening, and pressing together.

Adaptations:

1. Older children may have their sculptures fired. They can then be glazed and refired for permanency and an exciting finished product.

2. Use animal sounds to paint a mural in the school corridor. Play the tape of animal sounds as children walk by.

3. Make a panorama (a three-dimensional scene) with animal sculptures placed in their natural habitat. For example, wild animals in a jungle, domesticated animals on the farm.

4. Put on a play about animals, making animal masks to be worn by the children during the play.

LESSON 4: STORMY WEATHER! CONSTRUCTING A SLIDE STRIP AND TAPE RECORDING ON STORMS

A rainy day brings out rubbers, umbrellas, and other rain gear. It brings about puddles and reflections, but it also brings out RAINY DAY SOUNDS.

Tools, Materials and Equipment:

Wax crayons	Drawing paper
Clear and colored plastic	Permanent felt-tipped marking pens
Slide projector and slides, if desired	Tape recorder and tapes
Scissors	Filmstrip projector
	Rulers

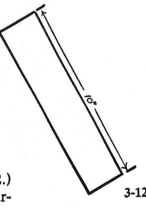

3-12

Preparation:

Cut clear acetate strips into pieces 1-⅜" x 10" (Figure 3-12.) or longer if desired (one piece per child). Plastic can be purchased, but much scrap plastic is available. For example, the clear plastic tops from stationery or other boxes are excellent for this activity.

Talk about recorded sound that we hear on tapes, records, television, and radio. Show slides or pictures of stormy weather.

Developmental Procedure for Activity:

Record weather sounds on tape, such as: thunder, hail and rain. Let children guess what each sound is by having them write a description of the sound and the object that made it.

Think about rain: how it looks from inside looking out a window; how it feels when it comes down on you; how it clogs your eyeglasses and drips off your nose. What do puddles look like? What shape are they and why are there reflections in the puddles? What do the reflections reflect? How would you show rain and reflections? (Children will have many, many answers to these questions.)

Now think about the sounds of a rainy day. How does rain sound: on a window, a roof, a car, on the street? How does it sound on an umbrella? (Figure 3-13.) or when a car speeds through it? or a child splashes in it? How does it sound when rain comes rushing down through a drain pipe? *How does rain SOUND?* and how could you show it on paper?

Try drawing rainy day sounds with crayons. Make your mind really remember the sounds!

3-13

Now make a film strip. Allow 2″ at the beginning and end of the strip, and divide the central area into sections ¾″ in depth (Figure 3-14.) and in each section show something you

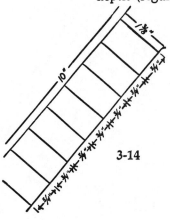

3-14

3-15

feel represents a rainy day sound. Would lightning make you hear in your mind a rainy day sound? Use the permanent felt-tipped markers to draw on the plastic and to fill in the colors. (Figure 3-15.)

Make a tape of appropriate sounds that can be played as each sound filmstrip is projected on the screen. Actually the sounds may be mimicked by the children, made up by them, or actually taped from the real natural source. Children will be enchanted when they see their drawings enlarged on the screen.

Specific Skills and Concepts To Be Learned:

1. Sound can be symbolized in line and color.
2. Permanent felt-tipped markers are good tools for drawing on plastics.
3. Completed drawings can be enlarged with a film strip projector.

Adaptations:

1. Make sound compositions by using felt markers, drawing on large sheets of clear plastic, and hanging on or near the windows.

2. Try gluing colored slips of plastic onto the acetate background in addition to the use of the felt markers, to make brighter film strips.

LESSON 5: RECORDS ARE IN!
DESIGNING AN ALBUM COVER

Album covers show the sound that the record inside will produce. The record cover is an art form, too.

Tools, Materials and Equipment:

Felt markers	Tempera paint
Scrap paper	Pencil
Construction paper or	Records
Bristol board	Record player

Preparation:

Discuss man-made sounds, some of which are recordings. What are some other man-made sounds? Sounds may be made by machines, by clattering dishes, pots and pans, by the actions of men and women performing the duties of their vocations, such as: hammering, sawing, and drilling.

Play some records and look at their covers. What is shown on a cover? What is the purpose of a cover? To protect the record? To sell the record? To give basic information about who composed the music, wrote the words, sang, played, published? How does the cover relate to the record?

Album covers have now become an art form, very similar in many aspects to posters. Today as much care is given the jacket as what's inside. Today's musicians want the visual effect of the cover to say the same things as the words and music inside.

3-16

Developmental Procedure for Activity:

Inasmuch as album covers and posters are very similar with regard to their basic construction, and since this background information was given in this chapter, in *Lesson 1, City Sounds Vibrate!*, only the basic instructions for making a record cover will be presented here.

Select a record and sketch (on scrap paper) a few simple designs for a cover. Select the one that is most satisfactory and transfer the design onto a 12" x 12" sheet of paper (the size of a record folder). Paint with tempera. (Figure 3-16.) Allow to dry thoroughly and then, very lightly pencil in the lettering and complete with felt-tipped markers (Figure 3-17.) Stress that the covers must be original and must dramatize the theme of the music itself.

3-17

Specific Skills and Concepts To Be Learned:

1. The record cover is an art form that describes the sounds to be heard from using the record within it.
2. Record covers sell the record, so they must appeal to the purchaser.

3. The design of a cover must conform to the size of the record or album. This affects the art work done on the cover.

Adaptations:

1. Write some of the children's favorite song titles, classic and/or modern, on the chalkboard. Then have them illustrate these, or make covers for the records.

2. Make up song titles and illustrate them. This is very good for the primary grade youngster . . . . . stirs his imagination . . . . improves his drawing . . . . . and correlates art and music.

LESSON 6: THE SOUND OF COLOR!
MAKE SLIDES THAT REPRESENT SOUNDS
WITH COLOR

Brightness and dullness in color visually represent loudness and softness in sound. This lesson helps children relate color and sound.

Tools, Materials and Equipment:

Slide mounts, 35mm, double frame	Colored construction paper
Clear and colored plastic	Slide projector
Scissors	Permanent felt-tipped markers
Model cement	Fluorescent paper

Preparation:

Spread pieces of colored construction and fluorescent paper all over a table. Ask children: Do you see, on this table, a color that sounds loud in your mind? One that is quiet? Is there a color that seems shrill? Is there one that seems high or low? *Are there colors that seem to make sounds?*

Now compare pairs of colors. Try the same sized pieces of paper in bright red and light blue: which sounds louder? Why?

Try bright red and fluorescent blue; that's a hard one. Fluorescent red and dark blue. Continue this kind of comparison with various hues, of different degrees of brightness. Try comparing colors in paper of different sizes. Does it affect the sound properties? *Keep relating different kinds of sounds with different colors.*

Display the work of artists who represented sound and music with color, line and form in their paintings. Piet Mondrian did *Broadway Boogie-Woogie*, where colors dance over the canvas. Wassily Kandinsky's paintings show many kinds of color sound effects. Giorgio De Chirico's work is very quiet, eerily so. Joan Miro's work tinkles with music. One must remember, though, that to hear the visual artists' sounds, the viewer must be tuned in. How does he become tuned in? By studying and looking at the paintings!

Developmental Procedure for Activity:

Make 35 mm slides that will demonstrate the concept that color has sound as was just developed under "Preparation" above. The following ideas may be used:

1. Create slides that represent separate sounds, using only one color on the slide to represent one sound, e.g. a slide with all red shapes making a loud sound.

2. Make slides with sounds using many colors to show an overall effect such as pale red and dull gray, making a quiet, almost muted total sound.

3. Make slides where more than one kind of sound is represented. (Red and pale green together to represent a harsh, shrill sound with a gentle, soft sound.)

The background of the slides is to be made on a plastic rectangle, cut to 1 ' 1/2 " x 1 '3/8 ", with two pieces required for most of the slides. Either of the following two methods may be used for applying the design to the plastic background.

1. Draw directly on the rectangle, using felt pens to fill in the lines and colors desired. (Figure 3-18.)

2. Use small pieces of colored plastic or cellophane and attach to the clear plastic rectangle. Place another piece of the clear plastic over the first one and gule in place. Be sure to use a very, very tiny spot of model cement when gluing, for too much

3-18

will melt or dissolve the plastics, causing the slide to curve and jam up the projector. (Figure 3-19.)

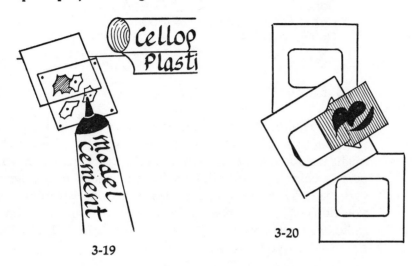

3-20

3-19

Insert the designs in a slide holder (Figure 3-20) and have a show of the "Sound of Color," letting the children read the sounds shown on the slides.

Specific Skills and Concepts To Be Learned:

1. Color and sound have a common denominator.
2. Sound can be interpreted into color.
3. 35 mm slides can be made with colored plastic, cellophane and/or permanent felt markers.

Adaptations:

1. Combine plastic colors and markers in one slide.
2. Cut up old film. Scratch it, punch holes in it and experiment with the making of sound color slides from it.

LESSON 7: UNWANTED SOUNDS ANNOY!
PAPER SCULPTURE DESIGNS

Annoying sounds abound in the American culture. This lesson shows how to make a picture of these using the techniques of paper sculpture.

Tools, Materials and Equipment:

Scissors   Cotton
Construction paper   Sponge
Rubber cement   Razor blade and/or
                                  X-Acto knives

Preparation:

Think about annoying sounds; sounds that you really don't like, that make you feel grouchy or even angry or violent. These might include the roar of a motorcycle, crackling candy wrappers in church, water dripping from a faucet, men collecting garbage early in the morning when you're on vacation, music you don't like, your baby sister crying, or even static on the radio. Annoying sounds are very personal, i.e., "I may like a sound which you find annoying."

Developmental Procedure for Activity:

Select a sound you could do without and make it into a three-dimensional cut paper design, letting some of the parts stand out. Three-dimensional paper work is called paper sculpture. It has height, width and depth, or three dimensions. (Figure 3-21.)

How does one make paper stand out? Try the following:

3-21

1. Place small paper springs, tiny bits of cotton or sponge behind the part that is to stand out. (Figure 3-22.)
2. Use scoring. Open up a pair of scissors and with a single blade, gently make a very slight cut in the paper. Bend away from the cut to make it three-dimensional. (Figure 3-23.) Older children may use a single-edged razor blade or an X-Acto knife, but these are very sharp and frequently cut through the paper (and sometimes fingers).

Glue the paper objects on a different colored construction paper for background. Does it convey the feeling of an unwanted sound? If not, add or take away something until your message comes through. (Figure 3-24.)

When finished, rub off the excess rubber cement with your fingers. Paper sculpture must always look clean with no excess adhesive showing.

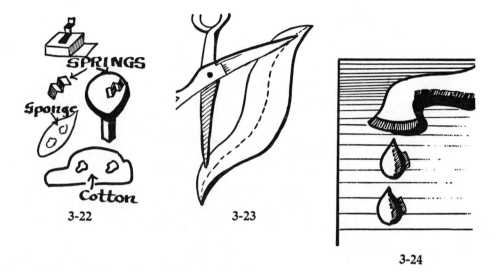

3-22

3-23

3-24

Specific Skills and Concepts To Be Learned:

1. Sounds are not always pleasant. Many annoy us.
2. Paper sculpture is used to create three-dimensional art, that has height, width and depth.
3. Three-dimensional objects can be made by putting something (spring, sponge, cotton) behind the object to make it stand out.
4. Excess rubber cement can be rubbed off with the fingers.

Adaptations:

1. Use the same theme and approach as was used in this lesson but make a two-dimensional design. This has only height and width, but no depth, and is a simpler concept for the very young child.

2. Make three-dimensional posters on unwanted sounds and their effect on the ecology.

LESSON 8: CREATING SOUND MAKERS! CONSTRUCTING SIMPLE MUSICAL INSTRUMENTS AND SOUND EFFECTS

Sounds can be made with everyday objects. Use anything that vibrates!

Preparation:

This lesson is divided into five sections, each based on generalized kinds of sound makers. However, those presented herein are only the beginning. Invent more! Be imaginative and experimental! There are more sounds that can be made than any teacher's head will be able to absorb.

All of the following sound makers can be decorated as desired. They can be painted, drawn on with markers, chalk and crayons. Glitter and cut paper can be glued on. Ceramics can be glazed or stained. This part of the lesson, therefore, will be left to the discretion of the teacher and the class, since the possibilities are endless and too lengthy to be included in this book.

Blow Instruments

Tools, Materials and Equipment:

Sharp knife	Bleach bottles
Tissue paper	Paper towel cylinders
Wax paper	Rubber bands
Construction paper	Comb
White glue	

Developmental Procedure for Activity:

3-25

1. *Make a megaphone* from a cut-down bleach bottle, using top section. (A sharp knife makes this job easier for the teacher.) Save the bottom for use as a disposable container. (Figure 3-25.)

2. *Using a paper towel tube,* cover one end with a piece of tissue paper, stretched tightly and held in place with a rubber band. Cover the other end partly with wax paper also held in place with a rubber band. A small place should be left open. (Figure 3-26a.) *Hum* into this open space to make the wax paper vibrate. (Figure 3-26b.)

3. *Cover a comb* with a piece of tissue paper and make sounds by blowing through the paper. (Figure 3-27.)

4. *Make a paper horn* by rolling a piece of paper into a cylinder and pasting. (Figure 3-28a.) Roll another piece of paper

3-26

3-27

3-28

into a cone shape and paste down. Cut off point. (Figure 3-28b.) Cut 1" slashes in one end of cylinder. (Figure 3-28c.) Bend these back. Glue the cone into the cylinder. (Figure 3-28d.) Child blows into the other end.

Rhythm Beating Sounds

Tools, Materials and Equipment:

Bottles	Silverware
Hollow objects	Rubber scraps
Paper	Cloth
Bleach bottles	Paper towel rolls
Metal rods	Tin can lids
Stapler	Wooden sticks, beads, spools, and/or blocks.

Developmental Procedure for Activity:

1. *Fill bottles with water*, at varying levels, and tap with a stick or piece of silverware. (Figure 3-29.)

2. *Use hollow objects to beat out rhythms:* pots and pans, pails, wooden bowls, plastic, and cardboard containers, as well

3-29

3-30

as coffee cans with and without lids. Special tops made from pieces of rubber balloons, inner tubes, paper and cloth may be stretched taut over these objects. Then tie on tightly. (Figure 3-30.)

3. *Make a drum* by cutting off the top of a bleach bottle. Hold upside down between the legs and beat on the bottom with drum sticks or merely use the fingertips. (Figure 3-31.)

4. *Make clappers* by covering two small wooden blocks with sandpaper. Wrap around the wood, overlapping enough to staple securely in place. These are rubbed together to make noises. (Figure 3-32.)

5. *For a pair of cymbals*, attach spools to tin can lids. (Figure 3-33.)

3-31

3-32

3-33

6. *Drum sticks* can be made by using dowel sticks with or without spools or wooden beads on the ends, metal rods, pencils, broom handles cut to size, paper towel rolls, and ice cream sticks.

7. *Hit spoons* and other silverware together.

Shakers

Tools, Materials and Equipment:

Rice, beans, corn, pebbles
Paper plates
Needles and thread
Boxes
Pop tops
Light bulbs
Pipe cleaners
Bells
Masking tape
Stapler
Dowel stick
Aluminum pie plates
String
Wallpaper paste
Spools

Developmental Procedure for Activity:

1. *Make simple shakers* by using the following methods:
   A. Insert rice, beans, corn, or pebbles in a box and securely close with masking tape.
   B. Place pebbles inside two paper plates and staple or sew around the edges. (Figure 3-34a.)
   C. Insert a dowel stick into a box, secure with tape and attach bells to the outside of the box. (Figure 3-34b.)
2. *Make a tambourine* by punching holes in an aluminum pie tin and attach pop tops from soda cans, with string. (Figure 3-34c.)
3. *Make a maraca* (a Brazilian percussion instrument used in pairs) by covering an electric light bulb with four coats of papier-maché. (Figure 3-35a.) Let dry. Hit the maraca on a hard surface (to break the glass inside). The glass will make sounds when the instruments are shaken. (Figure 3-35b.)
4. *For a bell shaker,* put 12″ pipe cleaners inside the cen-

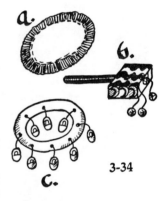

3-34

3-35

3-36

tral hole of a spool. Use enough pipe cleaners to fill the hole tightly. Attach small bells to the ends of the pipe cleaners. (Figure 3-36.)

Wind Chimes

Tools, Materials and Equipment:

Plastic coffee can lid   Nails
String   Ceramic clay
Kiln   Cord
Rolling pin or piece of broom handle

Developmental Procedure for Activity:

1. *Make a simple wind chime*, by punching holes in a plastic coffee can lid. Tie nails to the holes, making each close enough to the next nail so that, when the wind blows, the nails will hit each other and cause a sound. Attach additional strings to the top so that the wind chime can be hung up. (Figure 3-37.)

2. *For a ceramic wind chime*, roll out eight small pieces (2" x 1" or 2" x 2") of clay and cut into any simple shapes. Punch a hole in one end of each piece. Roll a large free form (peanut shape) about 6" long, punching eight holes around the edges, with two additional holes in the center. (Figure 3-38a.) Fire all pieces in a kiln. Attach cord to the two central holes, knotting the ends underneath. (Figure 3-38b.) Tie each small piece to a section of cord (about 5") and then tie into the holes around the edges of the free form. (Figure 3-38c). Be sure that the pieces are close enough to gently hit each other as the breezes blow.

3-37

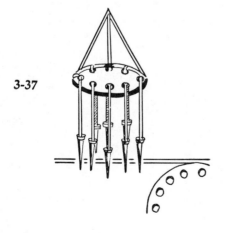

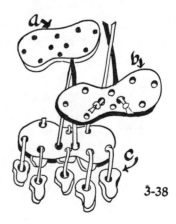

3-38

Miscellaneous Noise Effects

Tools, Materials and Equipment:

Pencil   Balloon
Corrugated cardboard   Glassware

Developmental Procedure for Activity:

1. *For an interesting sound,* run fingers or a pencil over corrugated cardboard.

2. *For a squeaky sound,* blow up a balloon, and holding the end, gradually let air out. (Figure 3-39.)

3-39

3. *For a ringing sound, or a dull thud,* use fingers to tap glassware. Note the difference in the ring of the sound, according to the type of glass and its method of manufacture. Try a piece also with a crack in it.

Specific Skills and Concepts To Be Learned:

1. Sounds result from a vibrating object.
2. Vibrating objects can be made from everyday materials and objects.
3. Sound makers can be made to be used in many different ways, i.e., blowing, shaking, rubbing, etc.
4. They can be decorated with art materials.

Adaptations:

All of the previously listed sound makers can be made more complex and beautiful by careful planning, longer work periods, and the child's ability to use complicated tools and materials. For example, a gifted child could plan and make a simple violin with strings. Older children could make ceramic wind chimes that have very aesthetic shapes and are glazed. Colored waters can be used in the bottle chimes.

4

Eyes Can Play Tricks

Our eyes tell us how objects look; thus, we learn to recognize them and increase our knowledge of the world in which we live. Our eyes introduce us to beauty as well as ugliness. This chapter deals with the visual sense and is concerned with the concepts that (a) our eyes have their own special reality, which differs from person to person, and from age to age, and (b) our eyes can and do play tricks on us.

Lessons will be presented for developing the ability to visualize, using habitual practice with art activities that concentrate on observations of living and inanimate things in school and in nature. We will be learning to look in order to see the environment as it is at the time we view it, and then to record it in our own special way, not seeking reality, but working from the concepts we extract from reality.

This is important inasmuch as the very young child does not draw what he sees. He may draw what he knows, what he wants to draw and what he can draw physically depending upon his eye-hand coordination and muscular development. He doesn't draw a tree the way it looks to him, but he responds to it emotionally. He may enjoy the feel of the crayon, so even though he's been looking intently at a cute puppy, he'll use the crayon for the pleasure it gives him, forgetting all about the little dog. He may or may not use color in a realistic way. If purple is his favorite color, his house may have a purple roof, purple windows, etc.

The young child is not able to draw an object with great facility, so he draws the object in his own way. All children, however, seem to go through various stages of development that are similar, regardless of their economic status, the country of their birth, their race, religion, or color.

For these reasons, the lessons in this chapter and throughout the book must always be used in accordance with the child's stage of development.

LESSON 1: FACES ARE FUN, BUT SO ARE BACKS! PAINTING BY LOOKING AT THE BACK OF A STUDENT MODEL

Don't be afraid of painting from a real live model. Get the feel of the paint, enjoy the free flow of the loaded brush onto the paper, and see what happens.

Tools, Materials and Equipment:

Tempera paint	Thick and thin brushes
Water containers	Newspapers
Drawing paper 12" x 18"	

Preparation:

Talk about how artists employ a person to act as a model while they draw, paint or sculpt the person's body. The model assumes various poses: sitting, standing, kneeling, and even lying down. In this lesson, we will paint a model from the back.

Developmental Procedure for Activity:

Select a student from the class. Pose the model in a comfortable sitting position . . . . . letting the other students see him from the back only. (The back view is easier for beginning figure studying, since there is no concern with features, only the body.)

Discuss how a person looks from the back. What can you see? Yes, his hair. How long is it? What color? Is it straight or curly? You can see his clothing. What colors are in his shirt? Can you see his arms? hands? What color is his skin? How does the chair look? What color is it?

Now select another student for a model so that the first model will have something to paint. (It's also a good idea to select a boy and a girl as the models.) Discuss how the second model looks from the back.

The next step is the painting process. (Figure 4-1.) Paint a picture of either model as you remember the pose or as you would like to paint him. Reality does not matter in this activity; simply paint a picture of a person's back.

4-1

Specific Skills and Concepts To Be Learned:

1. Artists use models to help them understand more about how a human body looks.
2. Looking at, and then painting, a picture of the back of a student model helps children to learn more about color and people.

Adaptations:

The media for this lesson can also be crayons, chalk or felt markers.

Older children, beyond the primary grades, may draw the model in the following manner:

Students will not be drawing with a pencil, but with a thin brush and one color of paint. Draw large, using the whole sheet of paper, drawing the entire body or as much as can be seen by the students from their positions.

4-2

Look carefully at the model and using a bit of imagination, search out colors. If, for example, a faint tinge of green is seen in the skin, use green. If the neck looks violet, paint violet. Do this for the whole portrait. Children will begin to see that SKIN can look like SKIN even if it is a different color from what one usually thinks it is. Keep stressing that there are many color tones in skin, not just SKIN COLOR. Use this same "searching by looking" approach with the whole body and the chair or table upon which the model is sitting.

Next go back and add colors on top of colors. Make one more intense or mix several by painting over colors. When the body has been completed, paint in a background using a thick brush. (Figure 4-2.)

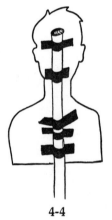

4-3

4-4

4-5

LESSON 2: MYSELF PUPPETS!
CONSTRUCTING SELF-PORTRAIT STICK PUPPETS

Draw a picture of yourself, add a stick, and you have a Myself Puppet that's just fine for a classroom puppet show.

Tools, Materials and Equipment:

Manila paper, 9" x 12"	Masking tape
Oak tag, 9" x 12"	Stapler
Crayons	Scissors
Pencils	Tree twigs

Preparation:

Request children to bring in tree twigs. Cut the twigs to a length of 12", take off all leaves, break off the tiny twigs, keeping the strong central one intact. (Figure 4-3.) This should not be too thick or it will be difficult to place inside the puppet. Incidentally, old rulers, pencils, dowel sticks, or even cardboard paper towel rollers may be substituted for tree twigs.

Developmental Procedure for Activity:

Draw yourself exactly as you look today. If you're wearing a blue dress, draw a blue dress. If your tie has white dots on it, draw white dots on the tie. If you wear glasses, draw them. Make the portrait large. Make it fit the whole sheet of paper. The portrait, of course, can be of your head or a whole body picture.

Color in heavily with crayons; bright colors show up most effectively! Cut out and then trace onto oak tag. Cut out the oak tag (which is actually the back of the puppet) and tape twig securely to it. (Figure 4-4.) Place the manila paper portrait on top, and staple around the edges. (Figure 4-5.)

Specific Skills and Concepts To Be Learned:

1. A self-portrait is a picture of the artist.
2. A self-portrait can be of a head or a complete body.
3. Stick puppets are one of the simplest forms of puppetry.

Adaptations:

Older children can study the self-portraits by master artists, such as: Vincent Van Gogh, Rembrandt Van Rijn, and Pablo Picasso. They can also make more complex hand puppets or even marionettes of themselves.

LESSON 3: CAN YOU DO A PORTRAIT OF A TREE? CHALK DRAWING OF TREES

In the last two lessons, we've been concerned with people portraits. Now try tree portraits.

Tools, Materials and Equipment:

Drawing paper, 12" x 18"   Chalk
Slides or reproductions
    of paintings showing trees.

Preparation:

Trees are spotlighted, in this lesson, for our special interest, careful concentrated looking and then for remembered drawings.

Begin the lesson by looking at paintings of trees. See the work of Monet, Cezanne, Van Gogh and others who have made pictures of trees that are distinctively unique. How do they differ? What colors are used in the trees, and in the trunks and bark of the trees?

Developmental Procedure for Activity:

Learning to look for your own personal reality can be strengthened by walking outdoors where there are so many objects that are useful for inspiration and observation. On a nice day, go outdoors and look for unusual trees. Why is this tree different from all the other trees? Is it not similar to the idea that each child is different from all other children! (Figure 4-6.)

Relate the tree to a person's portrait by considering the tree's trunk to be its body, the limbs to be arms, the leaves to be hair and the bark to be skin. (Figure 4-7.)

4-6

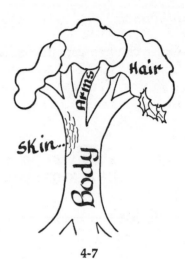

4-7

Now go back to the classroom and draw tree pictures. Use chalk for drawing as many trees as you desire. They can be different, or all the same. Use whatever colors you feel are needed for your particular, unique picture. If you'd like, when you finish the tree portraits, you may fill in the ground, sky and any other objects you feel should be around the trees.

Specific Skills and Concepts To Be Learned:

1. Trees have individual characteristics.
2. Careful, concentrated observation is helpful in learning how trees look and in drawing their portraits.

Adaptations:

All elementary school children can participate in this experience; however, the time spent by the very young will have to be considerably less than for the older child. Also, the teacher must expect that the young child's drawings will represent his particular stage of development.

Upper elementary grade children can make drawings of trees by working outdoors and drawing them as they look from different positions.

LESSON 4: FELT MARKER DRAWINGS OF PENCILS! DRAWING A PICTURE OF PENCILS

Did you ever take a tool apart mentally, and visually record its separate pieces? Did you ever look at one pencil and draw several like it?

Tools, Materials and Equipment:

Pencils   Large Felt-tipped markers
Drawing paper, 12" x 18"

Preparation:

Continue stressing careful scrutiny of objects in and out of the classroom, pointing out not only the object itself, but its various parts.

Show several different pencils to the children: short or long; with or without erasers, or with worn erasers; round, flat, hexagonal; colored or black; fat or thin. Pass them around, having the children scrutinize each pencil and its parts. Talk about them, too.

Developmental Procedure for Activity:

Suggest that children draw a picture of pencils, using large felt-tipped markers. Draw them really big if you wish. Draw a lot of pencils or draw only parts of the pencil. They can be SEPARATE AND ENLARGED. (Figure 4-8.) Fill up the paper, if you wish, with pencils. Then color in the background with a felt-tipped marker. (Figure 4-9.)

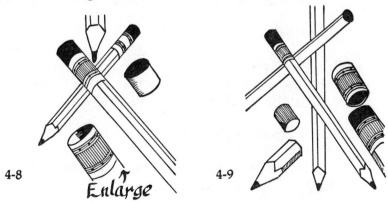

4-8   *Enlarge*   4-9

Specific Skills and Concepts To Be Learned:

1. A pencil is composed of different parts.
2. Pencils look different from each other.

Adaptations:

Try looking at, and drawing, other familiar art and classroom tools. For example, draw a stapler, pencil eraser, a paper punch and even a pencil sharpener.

Older children can draw the parts of a stapler: its top, bottom, staples and the section that holds the staples. (Figure 4-10.)

4-10

LESSON 5: CAN YOU SEE THROUGH YOUR HAND? SIMPLE OPTICAL ILLUSION CONSTRUCTIONS WITH PAPER, CUBES AND CYLINDERS

Fascinating tricks can be performed by using optical art. Children will respond with delight as they envision themselves to be art magicians, fooling those who will look at their creations.

Tools, Materials and Equipment:

Felt-tipped markers	Pictures or slides of Op Art
Tempera paint	Pencils
Brushes	Rubber bands
Water containers	White glue
Newspapers	Oak tag
Red and green cellophane	Scissors

Preparation:

Study some of the works of noted Op artists to see how they make the viewer see things that are not there; Josef Albers, Bridget Riley, Victor Vasarely, Richard Anuszkiewicz.

Developmental Procedure for Activity:

The following simple Op Art experiences can be used in the classroom to teach visual awareness:

1. See Through Your Hand:

Paint designs on cylinders made by rolling oak tag and gluing together. Let dry.

Do you think you can see right through your hand? No? Well, look through the tube with one eye, keeping both eyes open. Place one of your hands beside the tube, not too far from the top. You'll see a hole, the same size as the tube, right through your hand. (Figure 4-11.)

4-11

2. Make the World Look Red and Green:

Make two small oak tag tubes. Attach red cellophane over the end of the one and fasten with white glue. Hold in place with a rubber band until glue dries. Use green cellophane and attach to the end of the other tube. (Figure 4-12a.)

Hold one tube in front of each of your eyes (with the cellophane at the opposite end) and look outdoors. If you hold the tubes apart for their entire length, you will see two scenes, one red and one green. If you move the cellophane ends together, you'll see only one circular scene, tinted with both colors. (Figure 4-12b.)

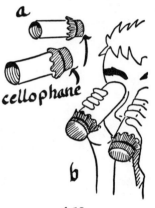

4-12

3. Which Card Is Larger?

On oak tag, draw two identical shapes as shown in Figure 4-13. Cut them out. Then create a geometrical design on each one. Fill in with felt markers. (Figure 4-14.) Now test your eyes:

Which of the cards is larger? Move them around; now which looks larger? Is it really? Your eyes are deceiving, for both shapes are the same size even though they do not look it.

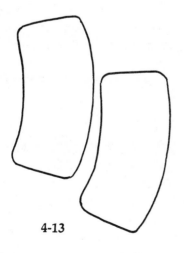

4-13

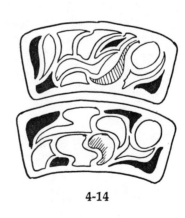

4-14

4. Color Tops:

Cut a circle of oak tag and draw designs on it with markers. Punch a hole in the middle and insert a small pencil. Spin the circle, as you would a top, and see the colors change. (Figure 4-15.)

4-15

Specific Skills and Concepts To Be Learned:

1. Our eyes can deceive us.
2. Our eyes work together to help us see the three-dimensional world in which we live, even though they receive two-dimensional images on the retina (the body's screen).
3. Spinning changes the colors we see.

Adaptations:

The concept of optical illusions can be studied in depth by older children; they can create geometrical forms, simulated movement, and even pen and ink patterns that fool the eye.

Older children may also try the following color cube:

1. Make a box that is a cube, with all sides the same dimension, as, for example, 4" x 4" x 4".

2. Draw squares that gradually get smaller until you have a tiny square in the center. Do this on all six sides.

3. Try various color schemes. Or try painting the different squares in colors ranging from light to dark with dark being in the center. Or try using only two colors, making every other square black and every other square red, until you reach the center. (Figure 4-16.)

4. When completed, ask yourself: Is the design going in or coming out?

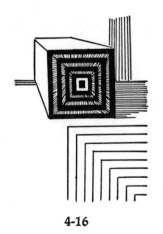

4-16

LESSON 6: IS A PERSON BIGGER THAN A CAR? ELEMENTARY PERSPECTIVE OF SIZE, COLOR AND PLACEMENT

Big and little; near and far! Toy cars are usually small, but a full-sized car can look as small as a toy, if it's far away. That's elementary perspective in a nutshell: giving a picture the illusion of depth. In this lesson, suggested for second and third graders, children are guided into an elementary perspective activity.

Tools, Materials and Equipment:

Construction paper	White chalk
Scissors	Photographs
Paste	Newspaper

Preparation:

Introduce photographs that show the near and far and discuss how the camera has brought a three-dimensional world (with height, width and depth) and duplicated it on two-dimensional paper (with only height and width.) The depth has been suggested by the photograph but it's not really there.

Depth in photography is caused by following natural phenomena:

1. Objects overlap one another. (Figure 4-17.)
2. Objects that are nearby appear at the lower part of the picture, while those that are far away appear high up or nearer the top. (Figure 4-18.)

4-17   4-18

3. Distant objects appear to be smaller than those near-by. (Figure 4-18.)
4. Objects in the distance appear to be vague, while

those in the foreground show much detail. (Figure 4-18.)

5. In colored photography, colors nearby are brighter while those in the distance are fuzzier, or duller. (The photographer usually focuses on a subject that will stand out, and he throws the background out of focus, to give it less importance.)

Many artists use these same concepts in their work. These are the basics of elementary perspective. (Note: There are other more complicated systems of perspective. They, however, will not be covered in this book, since most are too difficult for the elementary school child.)

Developmental Procedure for Activity:

Cut paper can be utilized to illustrate elementary perspective:

Give children a 12″ x 18″ sheet of green paper for a background and a 6″ x 18″ piece of blue to be pasted on the top for the sky. (Figure 4-19.)

For the remainder of the lesson, children will select their own colors as needed. It is advisable, however, to cut up a quantity of construction paper in 4½″ x 6½″ size, since this size should meet most of their requirements. Begin with the following exercises:

1. Cut out a tree that is large and one that is small. (Illustrates use of size.)

2. Paste the large tree at the bottom and the small tree nearer the top (on the ground, of course.) (Illustrates placement on the page.) (Figure 4-20a.)

3. Make two bushes, in different shades of green and paste down where desired. (Figure 4-20b.) (Illustrates use of color.)

4. Cut out two simple houses, in different colors, and paste one partly on top of the other. (Figure 4-20c.) (Illustrates overlapping of shapes.)

5. Make a person and show the features, hair and clothing in detail. Cut out another person in a much smaller size, and show no details. (Figure 4-20d.)

6. Now use white chalk and put a LITTLE on all objects that are far away, even the grass and sky. Blend in with the

Blue

Green

4-19   Paste

4-20

fingers, but DON'T OVERDO THE USE OF THE CHALK. (Illustrates dulling of colors . . . again due to the effect of the atmosphere.)

Additional interest may be added by inserting other objects into the picture (barn, animals, sun, flowers and birds).

Specific Skills and Concepts To Be Learned:

1. Photography shows us the natural phenomena of elementary perspective.
2. The basics of elementary perspective help us create the illusion of depth in our two-dimensional art work.
3. These tricks fool the eye by skillful use of size, overlapping, placement on the page, and vagueness of details and color.

Adaptations:

A wall mural can be painted by the middle and upper grade students, using elementary perspective. The same concepts can be employed on a nonobjective (unrealistic) painting, working to see if a large square at the bottom of the painting looks nearer to the viewer than a small square at the top . . . or if dull colors look farther away than bright colors, etc.

5

Taste and Smell to Learn

More About Our World

Many people feel that the sense of smell is the least used of the senses, but art teachers are very aware of the value of testing a medium by its odor. Are we using plaster or wheat paste? Smell them! They may look similar but they have very different odors. Has the ink or tempera paint gone rancid? Art teachers are notorious sniffers. Lost labels are unimportant when your nose has been trained to recognize the distinctive smell of the material contained in the jar. How do you get wet paint off clothes? You say the child isn't sure what kind he used? Sniff it. If it's oils, get out the turpentine. If tempera, soap and water will do.

Using the olfactory nerves, noses add to the knowledge we have learned from our other senses. How does an object smell? Is it fragrant . . . rancid . . . burnt . . . acid?

Closely related to the sense of smell is the sense of taste. In order to know what we are tasting, we often depend on our sense of smell. In fact, some illnesses, such as colds, affect both taste and smell.

Taste is made known to us by the taste buds located on our tongues. These help us classify an object as sweet, sour, salty, or bitter.

In this chapter are lessons that will lead the children through tasting and smelling art experiences involving art supplies and . . . even food. There may be problems, though! Some of the odors are so tantalizing they'll draw visitors with watering mouths into the classroom. Others may worry: "Why do I smell gas? Is there a leak?"

LESSON 1: BOTH GLUE AND MARKERS SMELL! GLUE RESIST DESIGNS WITH FELT-TIPPED MARKERS

Art materials *do* have distinctive odors. Discover for yourself by using your olfactory nerves.

Tools, Materials and Equipment:

White glue in squeeze bottles	Rubber cement
	Watercolors
Oak tag	Tempera paint
Newspaper	Model glue
Water containers	Food coloring
Felt-tipped markers: permanent, water based, and/or scented.	Pencils

Preparation:

The nerve ends behind our noses, up near our eyes, become chemically affected by the odors emanating from an object. By means of these nerves, any object can be categorized according to its scent. Some odors are delicate. Others are strong and overpowering. Observe this with felt-tipped markers. The specially scented ones smell delicious, while the permanent kinds usually are very potent and unpleasant.

Smell the paper in the classroom. Oak tag smells very different from newspaper. Why? Smell a ditto stencil. . . . or a mimeograph stencil. All are different.

How does glue smell? Is it different from paste? Some glues are dangerous to sniff (model glue) because they harm the body. Some have such strong odors that they have to be used with plenty of ventilation (rubber cement and epoxies). We can, therefore, conclude that all these adhesives, and other art materials as well, have distinctive odors.

The longer we sniff an object, the less we actually smell it. Why is this? Do we get used to it? Do these nerves behind our noses really change? Is there a reduction in the strength of the odor? Actually, the olfactory nerves can become tired and inactive if they are continuously subjected to a particular odor.

We are indeed lucky to have a sense of smell, for many

people who are old, or have damaged these nerves, cannot smell and their taste is often affected by the loss of smell.

Developmental Procedure For Activity:

Make a simple glue resist design as follows:

1. Draw a design using flowing lines, with pencil on oak tag.

2. Go over each line with white glue, using it as if it were a pencil, squeezing out a fairly thick line. (Figure 5-1.)

3. Let glue dry thoroughly. This may require one or two days, depending on the humidity and the amount of glue used.

4. Now use the various kinds of markers and color the glue lines as well as the spaces inside the shapes made by the lines. (Figure 5-2.) Notice how some of the markers will not write on the hardened glue, while others will. The glue resists the marker.

5-1

5-2

Try other glue resist techniques such as:

1. Drip rubber cement on oak tag. Let dry. Paint over the cement with watercolors. Let dry. Then rub off the glue with the fingers. The space where the rubber cement has been will now be the color of the paper. (Figure 5-3.)

2. Use the same approach as in the simple glue resist design on the previous page, except for the substitution of tempera paint thinned with water for the felt-tipped markers.

5-3

5-4

3. Mix food coloring with glue and proceed as in the lesson on the previous page. (Figure 5-4.)

4. Substitute model glue for white glue and proceed in the same manner.

Specific Skills and Concepts To Be Learned:

1. Markers and glues, as well as other art materials, have identifying odors, some delicate and some powerful.
2. The ability to smell decreases with sniffing time, with age, or damage to one's nose.
3. White glue, at times, resists the colored markers.
4. Various adhesives resist paint.

Adaptations:

This lesson is suitable for all age levels. The results will differ, naturally, according to the child's developmental stage.

LESSON 2: SPICES CAN BE PUNGENT! WORKING WITH SPICE-FLAVORED PAINTS AND GLUES

Paint with aromatic, pungent-smelling paint that delights the visual as well as the olfactory senses.

Tools, Materials and Equipment:

Spices, seasonings and leaves	Vegetable greens
	Plastic lids
Dill	White glue
Dill pickle pieces	Newspaper
Manila paper	Tempera paint
Watercolor paint	Water containers
Small brushes	

Preparation:

Collect various kinds of spices: Thyme, mint, garlic powder, basil, dill, pickling spices, sage, nutmeg, onion powder. Use mint leaves dry and powdered, or fresh. (Chew a piece.) Use fresh dill. (Taste a small piece of dill pickle.) Use the greens of carrots, parsley, onions and anise. (Chop up individually, and SMELL AND TASTE.) Have children learn to distinguish between the various spices and seasonings by their smell and taste.

Dilute white glue with ¼ cup of water to ¾ cup of glue. Pour into the plastic tops of coffee cans, one for every two children. Don't fill up too much for it's better to give the second small amount than to have it all over the table. (Figure 5-5.)

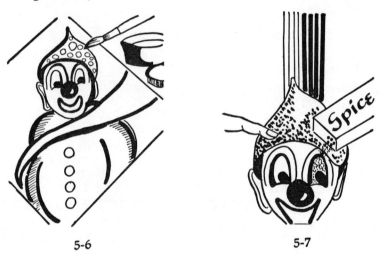

5-5

Developmental Procedure for Activity:

Try the following experiences with spicy smells:

Experience One:

1. Paint designs on paper using watercolors.

2. Go over portions of the painting with the glue solution. (Figure 5-6.)

3. Before the glue dries, sprinkle one or more spices on the sticky areas. Tap with a finger to press down. Let dry. Shake off excess. (Figure 5-7.)

5-6   5-7

4. While specific themes can be assigned (paint a clown), the aromatic paintings can also be unrealistic (just paint lines and shapes).

Experience Two:

Substitute tempera paint for watercolor paint and use same technique as described above. Do the spices still smell?

Experience Three:

Pour spice into glue and mix well. Then paint with the spicy glue.

Experience Four:

Mix spices according to color, i.e., mix a spice with a color of paint. Use another spice for another color. For example, you can paint with cinnamon brown that smells like cinnamon, mint green that smells like mint, yellow mustard that smells like—you guessed it—yellow mustard!

Specific Skills and Concepts To Be Learned:

1. Spices have distinctive odors.
2. Many plants have leaves and stems that are edible, and that have a distinctive taste and smell.
3. Some odors from paints (or glues) overpower the odors of the spices (or seasonings).

Adaptations:

These activities are especially valuable in the lower and middle grades but upper grades can correlate this lesson with science, testing out, and recording, the smells and tastes of various spices and seasonings, placing them within special categories, and then testing them again by combining with art media.

LESSON 3: GOOD AND BAD SMELLS AND TASTES! CREATING SMELL AND TASTE BOXES

Put your hand into a box and pull out a smell or a taste.

Tools, Materials and Equipment:

Baby food jars or pill bottles	X-Acto knife
Cardboard boxes	Smell and taste objects
Cloth (for blindfold)	Tempera paint
Water containers	Newspaper
	Large brushes

Preparation:

Discuss taste and smell.

Did you know that the tongue's tastebuds function according to their location? Buds at the tip of the tongue detect sweetness and saltiness. Those at the sides are sensitive to sourness. Bitterness is detected by those way in the back.

Smell and taste are related. Without a sense of smell, food is less appetizing and tastes different. As previously stated, in another lesson, people who have lost their sense of smell frequently lose some of their tasting ability, too. Smell often attracts us to food, then taste takes over, with smell still working cooperatively with it.

But . . . smelling and tasting are not always pleasurable. Some objects taste bitter (persimmons); some smells are horrible (sewer odor, or rotten eggs). Some are appetizing (coffee perking), and some make you sneeze (mold, pepper).

Developmental Procedure for Activity:

Create smell and taste boxes as follows:

1. In the top of each cardboard box, cut a hole large enough for a child's hand to fit through it. (Figure 5-8.)

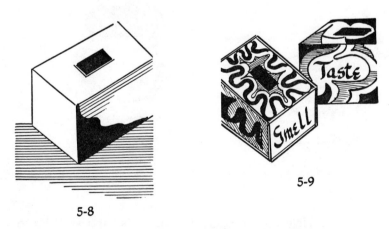

5-9

5-8

2. Decorate the boxes with tempera painted designs. Four children per box is a workable number, with one child being responsible for each side and whoever finishes first paints the top. Using a large felt marker, label some of the boxes TASTE and some SMELL. (Figure 5-9.)

5-10

3. For the TASTE boxes, place various TASTABLES in small plastic bags, write the name of the material on a piece of paper and staple shut. The TASTABLES can include: small amounts of cookies, fruit, vegetables, crackers, bread, cereal, spices, nuts, seasonings, instant tea or coffee in powder form and baking soda. Make sure all TASTABLES are kept fresh and clean. Small amounts of liquids or juices may be poured into a jar with a tight lid. Paste label on the outside. (Figure 5-10.)

4. The SMELL boxes are to use ordinary things in the environment. Place various SMELLABLES in small jars or pill bottles with tight tops. For example, soak a small amount of cotton in ammonia, alcohol, pickle juice, orange juice, vinegar, and place cotton in a jar. Or ... put in a bit of peanut butter, pepper, cheese, perfume, flowers, geranium leaves, after shave lotion, lemon juice, coffee, tea, vanilla, chocolate bits, rubber cement, wheat paste, ink, paint. All these can be used but a word of caution is necessary: BE CAREFUL NOT TO TASTE THOSE SMELLABLES WHICH ARE NOT FOODS. Bottle some good and some bad smells, and label each one. (Figures 5-11.)

5. Work with tasting by blindfolding a child. Have him puts his hand in the taste box and remove one item. (Figure 5-12.)

5-11

5-12

6. Help him to open the bag or jar and ask him to:

Taste the item by placing it in his mouth and let it dissolve on his tongue. Analyze the taste: Is it sweet, sour, bitter or salty? What is the TASTABLE? Is it a pretzel, bread, coffee? Remove blindfold and let child read the slip to discover what he tasted.

7. Work with smelling in much the same way. Blindfold, remove an item from the SMELL box, open the jar and say:
Smell the item selected.
What is it like?
Analyze the smell: Is it pleasant or unpleasant?
Is it fragrant or does it have a stench?
What is the item?
Remove blindfold and let child read the label on the jar to discover if his analysis and naming were correct.

Specific Skills and Concepts To Be Learned:

1. Smells and tastes affect one another.
2. They can be pleasant and unpleasant, powerful and weak.
3. Tastes can be sweet, sour, bitter and salty.
4. Smells can be described as fragrant, pungent, putrid.

Adaptations:

Children of all ages will enjoy this activity. They can also make their own individual taste and smell boxes. Older children can do research on occupations for tasting and smelling products: tea tasters, chemists and others who work on the making of fragrances and imitation flavors.

LESSON 4: HEAT AND COOKING PRODUCES CHANGE IN ODORS! DYEING EGGS, MELTING WAX USE HEAT TO CREATE ART

In this lesson, we will be learning that changes in odor, taste and color result from the use of heat.

Preparation:

Collect fruits, vegetables, eggs, candles and old, long crayons. Crayons must be wax and have all wrappings removed.
Discuss how cooking and the heating process creates special odors and changes the object which has been heated. Remember the odors at the amusement park refreshment stands

. . . at a street fair . . . an outside barbecue . . . or a hot dog stand. Recall the odors of a fire.

Now try the following art experiences:

Experience One: Dye Eggs With Natural Dye

Tools, Materials and Equipment:

Eggs, hard boiled	Big pot and lid
Water	Pot holder
Vegetables and/or fruits	Large spoon
Cooking unit (kitchen range, hot plate)	

Developmental Procedure for Activity:

Eggs can be dyed with commercial dyes . . . or they can be colored with the solutions made by boiling any of the following materials for about twenty minutes. (Use a large pot with a lid.)

1. Tangerine rind (for orange).
2. Beets (for red).
3. Spinach, or lemon or lime rind (for green).
4. Onion skins (for yellow).
5. Red cabbage (for purple or gray).

As these fruits or vegetables are boiled, notice and discuss the odors (and the water's color). Which are pleasant smelling? unpleasant? How do you like the smell of boiling cabbage?

Now put the eggs in the water, while the mixture is boiling and watch the shells change color.

Experience Two: Melt Wax To Make Crayon Drip Paintings

Tools, Materials and Equipment:

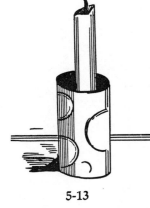

Peeled wax crayons	Newspaper
Cardboard, 9" x 12"	Juice cans
Old candles	Sand
Matches	

Developmental Procedure for Activity:

5-13

Cover tables with newspaper.

Fill juice cans half full of sand. Place a candle in each. One per child will be needed. (Figure 5-13).

Light the candles with a match and notice how the match smells. Hold the crayon over the candle and as it melts, drip it onto the cardboard. Drop spots of color over the entire surface, but be sure to stress the safe use of a lit candle. (Figure 5-14.) Notice, too, the smell of the melting wax. It's really not a pleasant odor, is it?

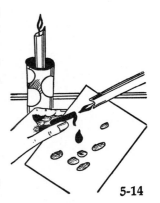

5-14

Specific Skills and Concepts To Be Learned:

1. Heat causes the odors of objects to change.
2. Heated materials, both foodstuffs and wax, have distinctive odors; some pleasant, some unpleasant.
3. Eggs can be dyed with the colors secured by boiling fruits and vegetables.
4. Crayons can be melted with heat.

Adaptations:

These experiences are effective for third grade and up. Younger children can be given a demonstration of the procedure. One or two children can work with a candle under the close supervision of the teacher with strict safety guidelines.

Older children can do all the work involved; younger children need help by the teacher.

Older children can go on to working on batik, which involves the heating of wax and the use of colored dyes. They can also become involved with making a precise design on the eggs, with melted wax, before dyeing in a colored bath.

LESSON 5: SAVOR THE COFFEE BEAN AND EAT THE PUDDING! PAINTING WITH FOOD

Unusual painting materials are always of value in learning about one's environment. Painting with foodstuffs is especially valuable, since they're tasty, smelly and unusual.

Tools, Materials and Equipment:

Liquid foods	Cotton swabs
Containers for foods	Drawing paper
Newspaper	Brushes
Water containers	White glue

Preparation:

All kinds of colorful liquid foods can be utilized for painting. Look around the kitchen and see what can be tried out.

Prepare all foods in advance, and pour into containers with tight lids.

Developmental Procedure for Activity:

Paint a picture using one or more of the items listed below (or others you may discover):

1. Instant coffee, mixed with a small amount of water.
2. Chocolate pudding, use when thin and runny or use in place of finger paint when thickened.
3. Mustard
4. Catsup
5. Chocolate milk or cocoa
6. Pea or tomato soup
7. Colorful fruit drinks or juice, such as grape juice.
8. Gelatin desserts, in runny, liquid form.
9. Runny frosting, made with confectioners' sugar, milk and food coloring. (When made thick, can be used to "paint" a cookie.)

Before painting, suggest that children taste and smell the food materials, analyzing each. Once painting has begun, NO EATING SHOULD BE ALLOWED, for the food will be contaminated by the brushes, the fingers and the painting process.

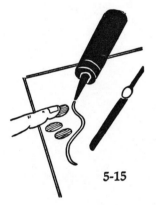

5-15

When ready to paint, point out the materials may be applied with brushes, the fingers or cotton swabs. They may also be applied by using a soft plastic squeeze bottle such as those used for mustard and catsup. (Figure 5-15.)

Also, suggest that:

1. Various tones and hues may be achieved by varying the consistencies. For instance, using more or less of the powdered coffee will make a darker or lighter brown.
2. Lines may be made very well by using the squeeze bottles. (Figure 5-16.)

5-16

3. These are temporary paintings, to be enjoyed during the process, to be used as a learning (and smelling experience, but to be destroyed shortly thereafter or the class may have an invasion of unwanted visitors!

Specific Skills and Concepts To Be Learned:

1. Foods are colorful packages of taste and smell.
2. They can be used for painting a temporary picture.

Adaptations:

This activity is applicable throughout the elementary school. Try adapting it, however, by using other household materials for painting.

1. Paint with toothpaste, shaving cream (on black paper), shoe polish, detergents (whipped with an egg beater).

2. Use bleach on colored construction paper, using a cotton swab as a brush. HOWEVER, use only with older children and be careful of eyes and clothing when using bleach. (It will take the color out of clothing as well as paper.)

3. Be sure to note the various smells of these materials.

4. . . . And, again, CAUTION CHILDREN TO TASTE AND SMELL ONLY EDIBLE ITEMS. . . .and SMELL SAFELY ALL NONEDIBLE ONES.

LESSON 6: FRUITS ARE DELICIOUS! FRUIT TASTING AND PRINTING

The school nurse will endorse this lesson since it entices children into eating good food for healthful living.

Tools, Materials and Equipment:

Fruit	Brushes
Knife	Drawing paper
Tempera paint	Newspaper
Water containers	

Preparation:

Give each child a piece of fruit and have him examine it closely. Become completely familiar with its distinctive characteristics such as shape, color, blemishes, skin textures, stem, smell, size, and weight.

Cut the fruit into sections. For example, an apple can be:

1. Cut in half horizontally (and see the star inside made from the seeds). (Figure 5-17.)
2. Cut in half vertically. (Figure 5-18).
3. Cut into quarters. (Figure 5-19).

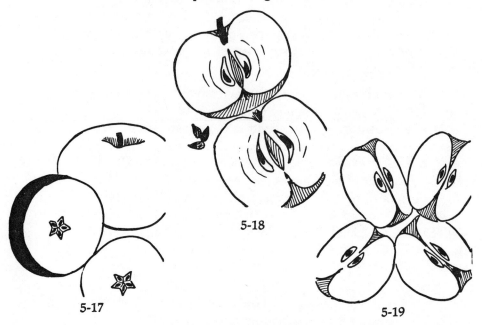

5-18

5-17

5-19

Smell and taste the fuit. Note how some fruits are sweet while some are tart, according to their natural flavor and degree of ripeness. Some are very wet with juice that runs out all over you. Some are quite dry.

Developmental Procedure for Activity:

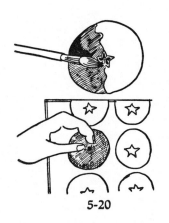

5-20

Make textile prints or wallpaper designs by printing with the fruit as follows:

1. Brush paint over a section of the fruit and stamp on paper. (Figure 5-20.)
2. Stamp rows of designs on the paper using the same section of fruit for the whole page.
3. Make other designs using different shaped sections of fruit or use various kinds of fruit.

See Chapter One of this book for introduction to printing, and additional details on the process.

Specific Skills and Concepts To Be Learned:

1. Fruits can be sweet or tart, wet or dry.
2. They can be cut into various shapes.
3. Fruits have natural designs within and without.
4. They can be painted and printed on paper to make textile and wallpaper designs.

Adaptations:

Use the same approach with vegetables. Print with an onion. Smell, cry and taste it, as well.

LESSON 7: SWEET AND FRAGRANT SCULPTURE! MAKING CANDY SCULPTURES

Candy sculptures are a sweet-tasting experience as well as a rather unusual way to create sculptures, even if they are temporary! How long can they last in a class full of children?

Tools, Materials and Equipment:

½ cup mashed potatoes	Commercially made candy
Powder sugar (1 lb.)	Granulated sugar
Fork	Food colors
Flavoring	Margarine, (1 teaspoon)
Large pot	Newspaper
Clean brushes	Cooking unit (range or
Containers for sugar	hot plate)

Preparation:

Bring in the materials listed above as well as some ready-made candy that can be stuck together to make sculptures. (Children may wish to do some of these at home before the lesson.)

Developmental Procedure for Activity:

Experience One:

Make a sculpture by using commercially made candy, such as mints, gum drops, marshmallows, Life Savers, hard candies,

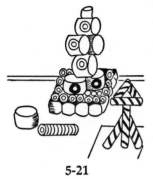

5-21

etc., and glue made by mixing granulated sugar and water. Stick candies together, giving each piece adequate time to stick to the next piece. (Figure 5-21.)

Experience Two:

Make modeling candy as follows:

1. Peel potatoes and cut in small pieces. Place in a pot and cover with water. Boil until soft. Drain off water and mash with a fork in a large pot. (Figure 5-22.) Add 1 teaspoon margarine and a few drops of food coloring and a small amount of flavoring.

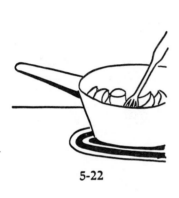

5-22

5-23

2. Stir powdered sugar into the warm potatoes mixture a little at a time, blending well. Add a bit more if needed. Chill for a short time.

3. Make tiny sculptures with the modeling candy using your fingers as the tool. (Figure 5-23.)

If desired, food color can be left out for white figures or after the sculpture has been completed, place a few drops of water and a small amount of food coloring in a clean container. The more water, the lighter the color. Mix and paint the sculpture with food colors.

Be sure to taste the sweetness of this sculpture.

Specific Skills and Concepts To Be Learned:

1. Miniature sculptures can be made from various types of candy.

2. Candy contains sugar and is sweet.
3. Food colors can be substituted for paint.
4. Food colors can be diluted with water and made lighter in color.

Adaptations:

1. Make sculptures from a pulled taffy recipe.
2. Pop some popcorn and savor the delicious aroma! Eat some! Glue some together into popcorn sculptures or popcorn collages. DO NOT EAT the popcorn with the glue on it. Paint the popcorn sculptures with Tempera. (Figure 5-24.)

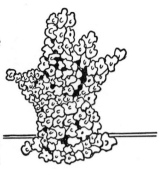

5-24

LESSON 8: VEGETABLES CAN BE BEAUTIFUL!
VEGETABLE COLLAGE CARDS THAT SMELL NICE

Celery leaves have a nice, clear odor and taste just as refreshing. When used on paper, they are an effective, fragrant medium for collage cards.

Tools, Materials and Equipment:

Celery leaves	Wax paper
Vegetables	White glue
Water containers	Brushes
Pinking shears	Construction paper
Scissors	Knives
Dish towel	Potato peeler

Preparation:

1. Clean vegetables and dry on a dish towel. (Figure 5-25.)
2. Have children taste and smell a small piece of each one.

Developmental Procedure for Activity:

Make a collage card by proceeding as follows:

1. Fold a piece of construction paper (9" x 12") in half, either horizontally or vertically. (Figure 5-26.)

5-25

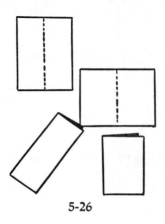

5-26

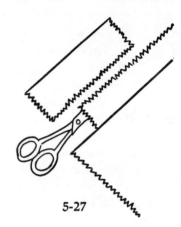

5-27

2. Make the edges look more attractive by cutting three sides with pinking shears. Cut along the edges, but not the folded edge. (Figure 5-27.)

3. Now arrange celery leaves and tiny, thin-strings, strands or slices of other vegetables as part of the design. THEY MUST BE THIN; so . . . cut with knife or use a potato peeler for shavings of vegetables. (Figure 5-28.)

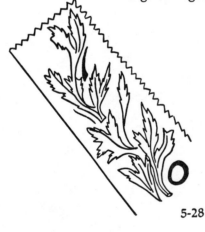

5-28

5-29

4. When the arrangement looks attractive, glue down with white glue. Cover with a piece of wax paper and weight down with a pile of books. (Figure 5-29.) This keeps the vegetables in place until the glue dries. Let dry thoroughly for two or three days.

5. Coat entire top of card with white glue. Cover with wax paper, books and let dry again. When completed, the glue will be clear and shiny with vegetables showing through the glazed surface. The celery leaves smell delightful on the cards for a long time after they've been made.

Specific Skills and Concepts To Be Learned:

1. Vegetables can be used to make collages, but they must be thinly sliced or peeled.
2. After gluing, weights must be used to apply pressure to make the vegetables remain in place and to help them dry out.
3. Celery's odor will remain with the card.

Adaptations:

Try this experience, using real flowers and leaves. Slice a bud thinly, or select real grasses (the thin, delicate kinds) and use for a collage.

Design Experiences

A work of art has a visual quality that is made up of the elements of design: line, shape, texture, color and space. The artist communicates his ideas by using these elements, combined with his perception through the use of his various senses.

Each of the elements is a part of all the others. They therefore should be studied together. Some of each will be present in each work of art. For that reason, the five chapters that follow will be very much interrelated, i.e., shape, texture, color and space will be used, often in a subordinate way, in Chapter 6, "Lines Have Character."

PART
3

6

Lines Have Character

In our everyday life, lines are used constantly. Lines tell us when we can pass a car (and when we can't). Lines on maps symbolize different kinds of roads and railways. We print and write with lines. Lines are in faces, wood and textile prints. There are lines of telephone wires and even clotheslines.

Did you know that lines do not actually exist in nature? They are, however, used in art to (a) depict the edge of a shape and (b) divide space.

There are many kinds of lines: horizontal, vertical and diagonal; curved and straight; open and closed; smooth and jagged; thick and thin; broken or dash and dotted; single and double. Textural and surface patterns are often expressed with lines. Lines may be made by using various tools such as a brush, pencil, pen, chalk or crayon—and even a pointed stick—as shown in this chapter. Each will be different, depending upon the tool used. Lines made by incising clay, linoleum and stone will differ, also, from lines of string, yarn and thread.

LESSON 1: FEEL A LINE!
SIMULATE A RAISED SURFACE WITH LINES

Lines can be felt and a surface can be made to appear different from what it really is by USING LINES.

Tools, Materials and Equipment:

Pencils	Drawing paper
Felt-tipped markers	Brown bags

Scissors   Paste
Newspapers   Cardboard circles
                                      Large coffee can of thinned
                                         red tempera paint

Preparation:

Lines can be felt. Cut brown bags into 9" x 12" sheets. Give one to each child, asking him to wrinkle it all up. Then gently smooth out the wrinkles, feeling the lines the wrinkles make. Wrinkle paper again. Dip into the coffee can with the watered-down red tempera paint. Squeeze out excess paint and let dry on newspapers, smoothing out wrinkles again, of course. The paint will be darker in the wrinkles . . . so children can now see the lines they felt.

In this lesson, the teacher stresses the seeing of lines as well as what lines do to paper.

Developmental Procedure for Activity:

Experiment with Drawing Lines:

1. Make a page of lines, using a pencil. Compare the page to a blank sheet of paper. Notice that lines give color or tone to the paper; it is no longer white.

2. Make a page of felt-tipped marker lines, and compare to the pencil-lined page. The marker lines create a darker tone than the pencilled ones. We can, therefore, conclude that lines change the color of the paper.

Draw lines on Top of a Textural Surface:

1. Place a sheet of paper over a textural surface, and draw lines on the paper. What happens to these lines?

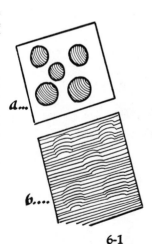

a...

b....

6-1

2. Paste cardboard circles on top of a piece of drawing paper. Five will be sufficient. Let dry. (Figure 6-1a.)

Turn paper over. Then using markers, at the edge of the paper, draw a straight line across, over the bumpy circles underneath, continuing until you reach the other side. Repeat this process all the way down to the bottom of the paper. Again you will have a page of lines, but these will have become a design since they will be affected by the bulges under the paper. (Figure 6-1b.)

Specific Skills and Concepts To Be Learned:

1. Lines can change the appearance of a surface.
2. Lines are affected by the textures under a sheet of paper.

Adaptations:

Older children may try the following for additional study:

Warp With Lines:

1. Draw very lightly, in pencil, several circular shapes on smooth paper. (Figure 6-2.)

2. Then using markers or drawing pens at the edge of the paper, make a straight line until you reach a circular shape. At that point, curve the line with the shape. (Figure 6-3.) Continue with a straight line to the other side of the paper, or until you meet another circular shape. The effect will be a design with straight lines and shapes that bulge in and out. (Figure 6-4.)

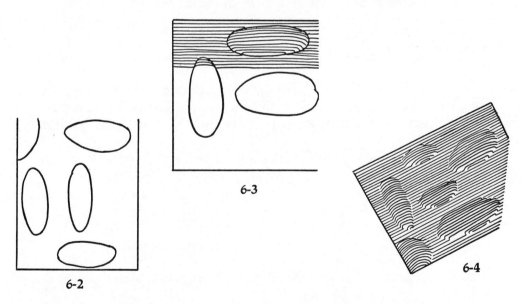

6-3

6-2

6-4

3. Use the same ideas as above, but warp the surface by using a checkerboard effect instead of lines. (See an example of Victor Vasarely.)

4. India ink may be substituted for felt-tipped markers.

LESSON 2: DRAW A LINE!
MONOPRINT A DESIGN IN A BOX TOP

Here's an inexpensive, uncomplicated form of printing.

Tools, Materials and Equipment:

Large flat gift box tops	Pencils
Finger paint	Brush
Finger-paint paper	Newspapers

Preparation:

1. Collect box tops, one per child.
2. Cut finger paint paper to the size of the box tops.
3. Discuss the graphic arts as an art form in which original prints are made. Monoprinting is one of the simplest of the graphic arts, and, as its name implies, means the making of one print from an original composition. Because of its simplicity, it can be done by the youngest elementary school child.

Developmental Procedure for Activity:

Using a brush (large size), spread a thin layer of finger paint over the inside surface of the box top. Keep fairly moist. Bumpiness of the paint adds to the textural quality of the finished pieces.

Carefully lay paper on top of the painted area and make a pencil drawing on the paper, pressing the lines into the finger paint beneath the paper. Try making all kinds of horizontal, vertical and diagonal lines. (Figure 6-5.) Textures can be added for interest.

Then pull the paper out of the box top and you'll have a line monoprint under your pencil drawing. This is an original print. It will be different from all other prints, even those made in the same box top.

Now as a second experience, brush on more finger paint to make a smooth layer of mushy paint in the box top. Use a finger and draw a line IN THE PAINT. Place paper on top of the drawing, pat lightly until you can faintly see that the design has

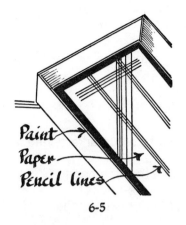

Paint
Paper
Pencil lines

6-5   6-6

transferred. Pull off the paper and there will be a print on the lower side. (Figure 6-6.)

If more prints are desired, add more paint, draw new lines, blot with paper and pull off. Each print is one-of-a-kind.

Specific Skills and Concepts To Be Learned:

1. Monoprinting is one of the graphic arts.
2. There are different methods of adhering paint to the paper.
3. In monoprinting, each print that is pulled is an original and will be different in some way from every other one pulled, even from the same surface.

Adaptations:

1. This lesson is of value to all grade levels.
2. It can be repeated in different forms, such as:
     Print with several colors of finger paint.
     Make lines with other tools, using sticks, combs, nails, clothespins, old ball point pens.
     Use glass, smooth scrap wood, a cookie sheet, lunch tray, or even linoleum as a surface instead of the box top.
3. Older children can use a brayer and substitute printing inks for finger paint.

LESSON 3: PAINT AND CUT A LINE!
MAKING PAINT AND CUT PAPER STRING DESIGNS

Lines can be made with paper and string as well as with pencils, pens or brushes.

Tools, Materials and Equipment:

String, cord, yarn	Felt-tipped markers, fine line
Scissors	White glue
Tempera paint	Construction paper, 6" x 9"
Paint containers	Popsicle sticks
School paste	White drawing paper

Preparation:

1. Pour tempera paint into juice cans, until about one-half full.

2. Cut colored construction paper into size 6" x 9", allowing three pieces of different colors for each child.

3. Demonstrate how string falls into ripples and it will only be straight if stretched taut.

Developmental Procedure for Activity:

Cut thin, wiggly strings from construction paper. Make one curved, thick line to attract attention and thus become a CENTER OF INTEREST. Paste carefully onto white drawing paper. (Figure 6-7.)

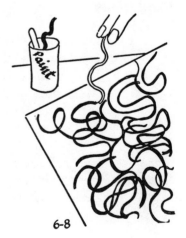

6-7   6-8

For a second experience, cut a piece of string about 10" long and dip into tempera paint, holding onto one end. (Use a popsicle stick to get it into the paint container.) Drop string onto drawing paper over and over and when necessary, reload it with paint. (Figure 6-8.) New colors can be introduced with additional pieces of string.

For a third, but still exciting, experience, combined paper string and real string can create an interesting design.

Specific Skills and Concepts To Be Learned:

1. Lines can be made from string; from thin pieces of paper or thick ones; and from painted string.
2. A heavier line, placed among thin ones, attracts attention and becomes a center of interest.

Adaptations:

This lesson is designed mainly for the primary and middle grades. For older children, try the following:

1. Drop a string on white paper and trace the design of the string with various colored fine line markers. Repeat this procedure until design is satisfactory to the student.

2. Manipulate string, cords and yarns of various colors and thicknesses on a sheet of colored construction paper until a pleasing design has been accomplished. Then adhere to paper with white glue.

3. Place the strings that have been dipped into the paint on newspaper and allow to dry in weird shapes. When completely dry, arrange interestingly and glue onto colored construction paper.

LESSON 4: DOODLE A LINE!
MAKE DOODLE CROWD PICTURES

Everyone likes to doodle—while on the telephone, in math class, or any place where there is a writing tool, a surface, and paper. In this lesson, circle doodles become a crowd.

Tools, Materials and Equipment:

Drawing paper, 12" x 18"   Newsprint, 9" x 12"
Pencils, hard and soft   India ink
Large, felt-tipped   Drawing pens
    markers

Preparation:

Talk about crowds. What is a crowd? A lot of people?
What kinds of people? What do they do? How does it feel to be
in a crowd? Where have you seen crowds?

Developmental Procedure for Activity:

Begin your crowd doodle by drawing circles all over the
paper, but never a circle inside a circle. They can be squashed
and flattened. They can be right next to each other, on top of,
or underneath, but be sure to fill the whole sheet with circles.
(Figure 6-9.)

Now change the circles into faces . . . all kinds of faces . . .
happy, sad; young, old; with hair and without; men, women,
boys, girls. Show how they look. How do people look in a
crowd? What can be done with these faces to make them look as
if they're in a crowd? Yes, fill in the spaces between them, with
parts of bodies that could be seen, or with more heads (or even
more lines). (Figure 6-10.) Can you recall seeing a crowd on

6-9   6-10   6-11

television? Sometimes some of them wave, or hold balloons, or placards. It depends on where the crowd is, and why all these people have formed a crowd. Is your crowd at a circus? or a parade? or in Times Square on New Year's Eve? Is your crowd at a riot? How would the people act? Complete your picture in such a way that we can tell where your crowd is. (Figure 6-11.)

Specific Skills and Concepts To Be Learned:

1. Doodles can be made realistic.
2. Faces can be made from circles.

Adaptations:

For additional study, try the following:

Young Children:

Make a combined doodle picture on a large piece of paper. Tape paper to the wall and label it with an imaginative title, such as: "He Tried To Eat Me Alive!" Allow children to work on it in their spare time. Let creativity have free reign.

Older Children:

Discuss the pencil and how there are various kinds made commercially. Drawing pencils are lettered with H for hard and B for soft. The higher the number imprinted on the H type, the harder the graphite (not lead) is. The higher the number imprinted on the B type, the softer the graphite is. Experiment with some of these hard and soft pencils. Begin your doodles with a hard pencil (which draws light lines). Then change, and use a soft pencil (which makes dark lines). Use a hard pencil to show light colors and a soft one to show darks.

Create pen and ink doodle crowds, keeping a crowd theme idea, putting in much detail, careful dark and light areas and even the use of large heads and small heads to represent the near and far.

Look at the doodle effects in some of the drawings and paintings of Jean Dubuffet. They are filled with puzzle-like pieces spilling all over the canvases, fitting together very tightly. all are outlined to separate them from each other.

LESSON 5: CURVE A LINE!
MAKE YARN COLLAGES ON WOOD

Colorful, heavy yarn can be used to make simple embroidery paintings on wood.

Tools, Materials and Equipment:

White glue	Brushes
Heavy yarn	White tempera paint
Scrap wood (6" x 6" or larger)	Felt-tipped pen
Scissors	

Preparation:

Prepare the wood:

1. Sandpaper to smooth and remove splinters.
2. Paint top and sides with a coat of white tempera for a light background.

Cut different colors of yarn into 6" lengths. Give ten pieces to each child.

Developmental Procedure for Activity:

Before beginning the creative embroidery, students should be shown the following procedure:

1. Designs will be simple.
2. Draw a line on the white surface with glue.
3. Place a piece of yarn right on top of the glue. Press down with fingers.
4. Draw another line with glue and press down another line of yarn on top, continuing this process until all the yarn is used up, or the design is finished according to student's desires. The entire piece of wood does not have to be filled in with yarn. However, if a student would like to have more yarn for his design, and would like to work longer, he should be allowed to do so.

Stress, even with the very young child, that an effective design must be simple, with an interesting division of space. It should not be too crowded, for a crowded composition is often a confused design. (Composition refers to the arrangement of lines, shapes, textures, colors and spaces.) (Figure 6-12.) Allow to dry completely.

6-12

Specific Skills and Concepts To Be Learned:

1. Lines can be made with glue and yarn.
2. Effective designs are simple and uncluttered.

Adaptations:

Older children may wish to try the following:

1. On scrap wood and using a black felt-tipped marker, draw a picture of an object such as a car, boat, flower or clown. Leave out details. Before beginning the creative embroidery, students must consider the object and how it relates to the size of the wood and its location on the paper. Is the drawing too small? Is it interesting? A class discussion on the drawings would be effective at this time. (Figure 6-13.)

2. Use only two colors for the whole design. These should be contrasting colors, with the option of using tints or shades of both colors. For example, orange and blue may be selected as the contrasting colors, with light and dark orange and light and dark blue used also.

6-13

3. The entire piece of wood is to be filled in with yarn. A small section is to be covered with white glue and filled in. Then another section is worked on until the wood is covered. (Figure 6-14.)

4. Allow to dry completely and finish by coating the picture with white glue, mixed with equal parts of water. (Figure 6-15.)

6-14

6-15

LESSON 6: DOTTED LINES!
MAKE A LINE DESIGN FROM RANDOM DOTS

Here are some line experiences for stretching the imagination.

Tools, Materials and Equipment:

Felt-tipped markers	Pencils
Crayons	Drawing paper

Developmental Procedure for Activity:

Try the following dotted line activities:

1. Close your eyes and, using a pencil, make random dots all over the paper. Open eyes and start to connect the dots using as many different kinds of lines as you can think of (short, long, straight, curved, zigzag, hilly, etc.) (Figure 6-16.)

2. Use another piece of paper. Place twenty dots on the paper. Connect all the dots with lines. Then see if you can discover a picture in the dots and lines. If you can, go ahead and add more lines and color in spaces to make it look JUST RIGHT.

3. Put one big dot in the middle of the page. Then place four medium sized dots anywhere near the big one and then six tiny ones far away in the corners or near the edge. Connect all

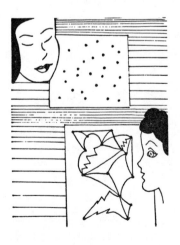

6-16

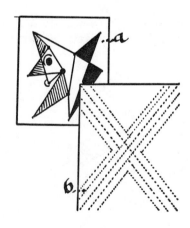

6-17

the dots with straight lines only and find a hidden picture in it. (Figure 6-17a)

4. A dotted line is only a series of dots. Make dotted lines from one corner to the opposite corner on the paper. Then do the same thing with the other two corners. (It will look like a giant X.) Now make a design from this using only dotted lines. (Figure 6-17b)

Specific Skills and Concepts To Be Learned:

1. Pictures and designs may be made with all kinds of lines.
2. Lines are the beginning of our drawings.
3. We can use dots and lines together in art activities.

Adaptations:

Young children may continue their use of lines by drawing art tools with pencils and/or crayons. Draw a pencil, a pair of scissors, a brush. These may or may not resemble the object.

Older students may go further in their study of lines by using the following:

1. Use wire as lines making animals and insects from wire lines.
2. Make contour drawings of pots and pans.
   A. Place pencil on the paper. Think of it as a tiny car, which will be traveling along the outer and inner edges of the objects we'll be drawing. Draw the car's path as it travels around the object.
   B. Look specifically at one pot. Really see the object, with its outer edges and inner contours. Select one contour on which to start.
   C. Looking at the object only, and with eyes avoiding the paper, travel slowly in your pencil car along one of the contours, letting your car make a line. Finish this contour and start on another. For example, you might start at the lower end of the pot's handle and travel all around the handle.
   D. Travel over all the contours of the still life. Let your hand record the car's trip with the pencil drawing on the

paper, and with your eye seeing and traveling along the pot's contours. (Figure 6-18.)

At first, these drawings will seem quite humorous, but with practice, some excellent, sensitive drawings will evolve, ones which will show the true essence of the pot. The eye, the hand and the pencil will learn to work together.

6-18

LESSON 7: STRING A LINE!
MAKE A SPIDER WEB DESIGN WITH STRING

Try combining string and chalk to make the lines of a spider's web.

Tools, Materials and Equipment:

Oak tag	White chalk
String	Needle, tapestry
Scissors	India ink and pen
White glue	Thread

Preparation:

What is a spider? Is it an insect? No . . . even though it's often referred to as one. It has eight legs, a body divided into two parts and produces silk from several spinnerets on its body. The silk is used to make nests, cocoons or webs for the purpose of trapping food . . . insects! Have you ever seen a spider web? . . . in the morning with drops of dew on it? Have you ever run into a web? How does it feel? How do they look? They're a series of LINES, woven in and out. Draw one on chalkboard.

Demonstrate:

1. Threading a needle. Use thin string about 30" long. Pull string so ends are together to make a double thickness. (Figure 6-19a.)

2. Knot the ends of the string together. (Figure 6-19b.)

3. When working with the needle and string, keep the knots on the back. (Figure 6-19c.)

Developmental Procedure for Activity:

Imagine you are a spider! Spin a web by drawing lines of chalk on oaktag.

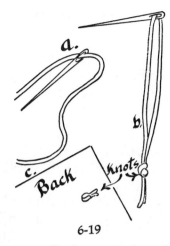

6-19

6-20

Use a needle (no string) and punch holes in the paper wherever two lines meet, and in between, about every inch, if the lines are long. (Figure 6-20.)

Thread needle and knot string. Start sewing from the back, at any place. Put the point of the needle through one of the holes and pull string out at the top. Then push needle into nearest hole and down into back of the design. Push up to the top again and back. Repeat this procedure until the whole web is covered with string. Other colors may be used and additional lines may be sewn wherever needed.

Specific Skills and Concepts To Be Learned:

1. Spiders are not insects.
2. They have eight legs and spin webs to catch their food.
3. These webs are natural works of art in lovely design.
4. Sewing a web must be done carefully or string will tangle.
5. Knots are necessary at the end of the string so that the string will not be pulled through the oaktag.
6. Needles have eyes, through which thread or string is pulled. This is called threading the needle.

Adaptations:

This kind of activity provides motor skill exercises and sharpens the observational and retentive powers of the student.

Other activities for the older child, that can be related to this line experience, are:

1. Draw spider web designs using pens and India ink.
2. Dip string in glue and adhere to chalk drawing of a web.
3. Embroider web designs, using thread, on an article of clothing.

LESSON 8: CAN LINES BE WHITE? MAKE BLACK DESIGNS WITH WHITE LINES

Lines created in this lesson are white instead of black, and are drawn by scratching off the top layer of the paper's waxy surface.

Tools, Materials and Equipment:

White and black crayons   Scissors
Thin dowel sticks   Oaktag
Newspaper

Preparation:

Think how lines are usually seen in black, but why can't they be drawn in white, or any other color for that matter? How many ways can you think of to make white lines: draw with WHITE chalk, WHITE ink, WHITE pencil, WHITE crayon on black paper. Paint WHITE lines . . . or make WHITE lines using scratchboard.

Developmental Procedure for Activity:

Commercial scratchboard and scratch paper can be purchased or it can be made by the students as follows:

1. Cover the oaktag with a thick coat of white crayon. (Figure 6-21a.)
2. Cover the white crayon with a thick coat of black crayon. (Figure 6-21b.)
3. Draw a design in pencil. Scratch through the penciled design into the waxed surface with a sharpened dowel stick, or a point of one of the scissor's blades. Scratch carefully and a

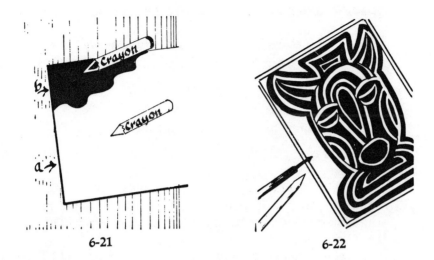

6-21   6-22

white line will emerge from the white crayon under surface. (Figure 6-22.)

Allow a lot of black surface to remain but create interest by:

1. Making multiple lines. (Figure 6-23a.)
2. Making textures of lines. (Figure 6-23b.)
3. Taking out complete areas of black, leaving a large white space. (Figure 6-23c.)

6-23

Specific Skills and Concepts To Be Learned:

1. Lines can be made by scratching as well as drawing.
2. They can be white as well as other colors.

Adaptations:

Adaptations to this lesson might include:

1. Drawing on black paper with white crayon, pencil, ink or chalk.

2. Older children may make a linoleum block with a line design carved into it. Print with black ink on white paper or white ink on black paper. In the former, the lines will be white; the latter will produce black lines.

3. Paint thick white lines on black paper with a Q Tip and white tempera paint.

7

Shapes Exist in Unlimited Variations

Children are surprised when the teacher states: "I have a shape. You have a shape. The desk has a shape . . . that lunch box . . . the flower pot . . . the sink . . . all have shapes."

Of many kinds, all quite different, shapes exist in unlimited variations according to size, thickness, weight, proportion, texture and color. The concept of shape itself implies that an object has weight, or mass, and that it is three-dimensional, having height, width and depth.

A synonym for shape is the word form. The overall structure of an object is its form, its outward appearance, which is based, of course, upon functional capacity.

In this chapter, children will create shapes with paper, chalk, newspaper, clay, flour and even snow.

LESSON 1: MYSTERIOUS SHAPES!
CUTTING PAPER REVERSE SILHOUETTES

Silhouettes are shadow portraits, usually made of black paper glued onto a white background. This lesson, however, presents some simple activities for making, recognizing and preserving white portraits glued onto a black background, since young children can see and cut lines on white paper more readily.

Tools, Materials and Equipment:

Black and white construction paper, 12" x 18"
Scissors   Projector or floor lamp
Pencils   Screen
Paste   Masking Tape

Preparation:

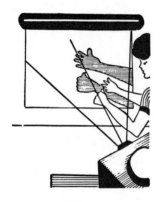

Become acquainted with silhouettes by using the following visual discrimination exercises:

1. Collect simple objects, those whose outlines will be easily identified. Include such items as: small statues, toys, fruits, vegetables, dishes, pots, paint brush, stapler, and even fingers.

2. Set up a screen with a slide or filmstrip projector. Turn on the lamp.

3. Hold one of the objects, in profile position, in front of the projector. (Figure 7-1.)

4. Ask pupils to try to name the object.

5. Then try another item.

7-1

Developmental Procedure for Activity:

Discuss the concept that a silhouette is a profile view of a shape showing outer edges with no details. Paper silhouettes are usually cut from black paper. However, in the procedures that follow, white will be used because it is easier to see a black line on white paper, than white or colored lines on black paper.

Instruct the children to cut a few silhouettes using the following methods, which require that they work in pairs, each taking a turn helping the other partner.

1. Leaf, Flower and/or Fruit Silhouettes

Place white paper on desk and lay an object on top of the paper. One child will hold the object, keeping it from wiggling, while his partner traces around it with a pencil. (Figure 7-2.) The child who traced the shape now cuts it out and mounts it on black paper. The same process is repeated for the second child.

This is an excellent activity for those who lack confidence, and for the very young child. It is a good beginning activity for learning to cut.

7-2

2. Children's Reverse Silhouette Portraits

Tape white paper to the wall. Set up the projector and turn on the lamp. Have the first child stand between the projector and the paper. The light will cast the shadow of his profile onto the paper. The second child now traces around the shadow with a pencil. (Figure 7-3.)

The first child cuts out, and mounts, his own portrait on black background paper. (Figure 7-4.) Repeat the same process for the partner.

7-3   7-4

3. Finger Figures

Finger figures are made by manipulating one or two hands in order to make a shape, either recognizable or abstract.

Fasten a piece of white paper to the wall. One child makes a finger figure in front of the projector, making certain the shape falls within the outer edges of the paper. (Figure 7-5.) His partner then traces the edges of the figure with a pencil. The first child cuts out his design and pastes it onto black paper. Repeat the process for the partner.

7-5

Specific Skills and Concepts To Be Learned:

1. Silhouettes are shapes, usually black, which show a profile view, and only the outer edges with no details.
2. Reverse shilhouettes are white shapes.
3. Objects placed in front of a light will cast a shadow on the wall.

4. Mounting a light shape on a dark background makes a very interesting design.

Adaptations:

This lesson can be used for young children as soon as they can draw controlled lines and can cut. Most kindergartners can do this by the middle of the term.

Middle and upper grades can make more complex silhouettes as follows:

1. Use silhouettes to illustrate stories and other subject matter, such as illustrating how people live in another country.

2. Draw freehand silhouettes, using any shape desired, on BLACK paper instead of white. Show only the profile and outer edges with no details. (Children will be tempted to put in details when they draw a freehand shape.)

3. Make colored silhouettes instead of black or white.

4. Make silhouettes on original paper, drawing on the white side.

LESSON 2: IS A TOOTH FAIRY A MAN OR A WOMAN? MAKING CHALK DRAWINGS OF TOOTH FAIRIES

Children all know the Tooth Fairy, but how many have seen one? In this lesson, he (or is it she) becomes a reality!

Tools, Materials and Equipment:

Chalk	Newspaper
Drawing paper 12" x 18"	Rubber bands
Pictures of teeth	

Preparation:

Discuss teeth: What does a tooth look like? What is its shape? What happens when you lose a tooth? Do you save your teeth when they come out? Talk about the Tooth Fairy. Who is the Tooth Fairy? A man or a woman? How would the Tooth Fairy dress?

Developmental Procedure for Activity:

Look at teeth: in your own mouth, the teeth of other children and pictures of teeth. What kind of a shape is a tooth? Are they all the same?

Now let's draw pictures of a Tooth Fairy. There are several ways it can be done. For example, we can draw from imagination or, in other words, draw how we think a Tooth Fairy looks. We can draw a Tooth Fairy with a body that is based on a tooth. This procedure is described below:

Using a light colored piece of chalk, draw a tooth upside down, with the prongs at the bottom. Make these prongs into legs. Add a head, arms, hands and feet. Give the Tooth Fairy a face, hair and clothes. Would this kind of a fairy be carrying a wand? a bag full of money? Remember that the Tooth Fairy does not have to be beautiful, female or elegantly dressed, or in any way to resemble reality. Simply make this Tooth Fairy look the way you think he or she actually is. (Figure 7-6.) You can also make the tooth the head and add a body to it with arms, legs, etc. (Figure 7-7.)

7-6

For another drawing activity, make a picture of the Tooth Fairy's home and community. Are there other Tooth Fairies or only one? Does he or she have a mother, father, or family? Where would the Tooth Fairy live? In your mouth? In a tooth? In the dentist's office? Out in the fields? Under a mushroom? Would a Tooth Fairy have a car, a bus or a plane?

Use your imagination and draw many illustrations that will help us know more about this interesting character.

In this lesson, chalk is suggested as the drawing medium. Draw first with a light-colored piece, for then mistakes can be easily rubbed out or blended so that there is no waste of paper. After the initial outline drawing is made, all shapes can be filled in with the various colors of chalk as desired by the students. It is well for the teacher to stress the following:

7-7

1. Chalk smears. For that reason, do not lean on your drawing.
2. Black chalk usually contaminates the whole drawing. Use it after you have finished with all the other colors.

3. A very small amount of chalk can be blended onto the paper to create a light color. Just put a small amount on the paper, and rub (or blend) with a finger.
4. New colors can be made by putting one color of chalk on top of another color.
5. Do not blow the chalk dust off the paper but tap it lightly onto the newspaper covered table.

When drawings are finished, they may be taken home by placing them carefully inside a double sheet of newspapers. Then roll and hold together with a rubber band.

Specific Skills and Concepts To Be Learned:

1. Chalk is a good medium for illustrating stories or themes.
2. Shapes can be changed into new shapes.
3. Chalk is dusty; it smears, blends and can be used to create new colors.

Adaptations:

This activity is especially fine for the primary grades when children are losing their teeth and know all about the fable of the Tooth Fairy.

For older children, let them try changing other everyday shapes into new shapes: Change a pickle into an insect. Change a walnut into a bird; a cup of coffee into a hat; a shoe into a car; a television set into a robot.

LESSON 3: EGG SHAPES ARE BEAUTIFUL IN THEIR SIMPLICITY! MAKE A RELIEF MURAL WITH COLOR BUGS

In this lesson, simple crayoned egg shapes are combined to create a mural on the concept of color.

Tools, Materials and Equipment:

Scissors	Black yarn
Oaktag	Sponges

Crayons	White tempera paint
Stapler	Project paper (Kraft paper or
Newsprint	wallpaper
Masking tape	Cut down bleach bottles
Pictures of Brancusi's	
"Eggs"	

Preparation:

The shape of an egg appears to be extremely simple, but it is aesthetically pleasing. Artists have worked with this beautiful shape for a long time. Constantin Brancusi, for example, created sculptures of unprecedented beauty in simplicity. One of his constant themes was the egg, which he used as an egg itself and as a head shape. The head with the features lightly but sharply cut out was presented in different variations in marble, bronze and plaster, and always it was polished, smooth and elegant.

To begin this lesson, show the pictures of Brancusi's work with egg shapes. Then discuss how we will work also with egg shapes in the making of a relief mural (a wall decoration where the parts stand away from the background). Each child will make a contribution toward the joint project.

Developmental Procedure for Activity:

The title for our mural will be "Egg-Shaped Color Bugs." If children haven't had color experiences, talk about the names of colors and how we find color in everything we see. For very young children suggest that they try to make as many colors as they can on a piece of newsprint. Then have them name each color they used.

For primary grades, talk about the technique of changing colors:

1. Make lighter by pressing gently, and darker by pressing harder on the crayon, or

2. Make lighter or darker by putting one color on top of another.

Let children experiment on newsprint:

1. Make light red, by:
    A. Pressing lightly on the red crayon, or
    B. Rubbing white over red.

2. Make dark red, by:

A. Pressing heavily on the red crayon, or

B. Rubbing a dark color (black, blue, brown) over red.

Try this procedure with other colors, too.

7-8

Begin the Mural:

Give each child a sheet of 9″ x 12″ oak tag and suggest he draw an egg-shaped color bug. First, make an egg shape to which will be added: legs, antenna, eyes, feelers, stingers, decorative design, etc. (Figure 7-8.) Color it with one color only. It can be a red bug, or a blue bug, or whatever color is desired, but it must be all RED or all BLUE. If it's a blue bug, it can be light blue, dark blue, bright blue, but it CANNOT have any red on it.

When completed, cut out the bugs.

Make the Background:

Paint the background paper by using a sponge and white paint. Pour paint into a cut-down bleach bottle. Dip sponge into paint and press onto background paper. (Paper, of course, should be placed on the floor on top of newspapers to keep the floor clean.) (Figure 7-9.) Continue pressing paint on paper until completely covered. Let dry and staple to bulletin board.

Staple some black yarn from one side of the bulletin board to the other. Have some yarn lines running in different directions all over the mural, somewhat like a spider's web. (Figure 7-10.)

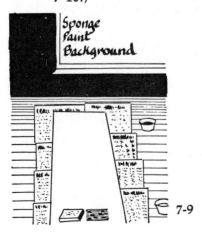

7-9

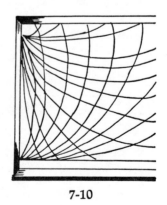

7-10

Arrange the Mural:

Roll tape and place several pieces on the back of the color bugs. (Figure 7-11.) Let the children place the color bugs all over the mural wherever they feel they should be. Arrange and Rearrange. KEEP MOVING THEM UNTIL THEY LOOK JUST RIGHT! Make up stories about them as you work. They can be used in a similar way to puppets. Talk for them. Keep changing their positions. Add new ones. (Figure 7-12.)

7-11

Specific Skills and Concepts To Be Learned:

1. Constantin Brancusi was a sculptor who worked with creating egg shapes.
2. His egg shapes were made in marble, bronze, and plaster but always polished, smooth and elegant.
3. A relief mural is a wall decoration where parts stand away from the background.
4. Crayoned colors can be made light, dark and bright, by pressing lightly or heavily, or by putting one color over another.
5. Sponge painting a background is a quick, pleasant way to make a simple mural.
6. An egg shape is simple but artistic.

7-12

Adaptations:

This mural is a simple activity, suitable for very young children. Middle and upper grades (as well as primary) may also make a Color Bug Mural, extending it to more detailed bugs, more detailed and complex surroundings, depending upon the ability of the children involved. Older children may make surroundings that can become a solid relief mural by placing a spring on the back and gluing down with white glue.

Also, the same theme, and simple shape, can be used with relief sculptures made of clay tiles, fired and glazed and permanently installed in the school.

LESSON 4: FLOWER SHAPES FOR
HANGING IN THE WINDOW!
USE PAPER CLAY TO MAKE FLOWER SCULPTURE

Pulp, or mash papier maché, a modeling medium quite similar to clay, is also very easy for little hands to manipulate.

Tools, Materials and Equipment:

Straws	Paste containers
Newspaper	Wheat paste
Water containers	Pail or large basin
White glue	Tempera paint
Plastic bags	Paint brushes
Cardboard (9" x 12" or larger	
Ribbons	

Preparation:

Mix the paper clay as follows:

1. Tear newspaper into small pieces and place in a large pail or basin.
2. Cover with warm water and soak for several hours.
3. Squeeze out excess water.
4. Sprinkle dry wheat paste over the pulp, kneading thoroughly until the paper clay is smooth and pliable.
5. If dough is not stiff, add more paste or water.
6. This clay will remain in a workable condition for several days.

Developmental Procedure for Activity:

Provide each child with:

1. A ball of paper clay about the size of an orange.
2. A piece of cardboard placed inside a plastic bag. The cardboard is the surface on which the flower shape will be assembled, while the plastic bag will keep the sculpture from adhering solidly to the cardboard. (Figure 7-13.)

7-13

Demonstrate how the paper clay can be modeled and made into various shapes. Suggest to very young children that they make something simple until they get to know how to use the medium. Simple shapes such as a ball, apple, banana, peanut are adequate for the very young child.

Primary grade children can be shown how to make sculptured flowers as follows:

1. Make clay into balls about the size of a large cherry. Press or flatten on top of plastic-covered cardboard. Flatten into petal shapes with ends pointed or rounded. Keep petals thick for sturdiness. (Figure 7-14a.)

2. A ball is made for the center.

3. All petals are placed around the center and then firmly pressed together. (Figure 7-14b.)

4. Make a hole in the top by pushing a piece of straw through the flower. (Figure 7-14c.)

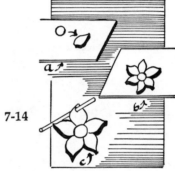

7-14

Place the sculptured shape in a well-ventilated location, allowing plenty of time to dry. Then paint with tempera. If a shiny piece is desired, paint over dry tempera with a coat of slightly watered down white glue.

Run a ribbon through the hole, and hang up some lovely flower shapes.

Specific Skills and Concepts To Be Learned:

1. Paper clay is a modeling medium.
2. Plastic keeps paper clay from sticking to cardboard.
3. Painted surfaces can be made shiny by giving them a coat of white glue.

Adaptations:

Paper clay can be made into all kinds of sculptural shapes and is readily usable on all grade levels.

LESSON 5: BASIC SHAPE FRUITS COME IN ALL SIZES! STUFFED NEWSPAPER SCULPTURE

Big fruits are fun to make and an excellent means of learning about basic shapes.

Tools, Materials and Equipment:

Newspapers	Wheat paste
Large felt markers	Scissors
Old nylons or stockings	Staplers
Paste containers	Tempera paint
Brushes	Newsprint
Crayons	

Preparation:

Collect newspapers and nylons.

Mix paste according to directions on the wheat paste package and pour into cut down bleach bottles.

Developmental Procedure for Activity:

Carefully scrutinize some real fruits. Analyze their basic shapes. A tomato is basically a ball or sphere. A strawberry is a cone; a banana is a bent cylinder. Oranges, grapefruit, cherries and grapes are basically spheres in different sizes. A pear is a big sphere with a little sphere on top. Draw these on the board, as the discussion progresses. Then make some quick drawings of basic shape fruits, using crayons and newsprint paper. (Figure 7-15.)

7-15

In order to make the stuffed fruit sculptures, it is recommended that students follow the steps listed below:

1. *Prepare Shapes:*

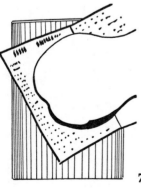

Open newspapers to fullest size and draw a huge piece of fruit (using a felt-tipped marker). (Figure 7-16.) Cut out six sheets of each shape, all exactly the same size. This can be done at one time if large scissors are used and IF the child is in third grade. Younger children will need either some help from the teacher, or plenty of time to cut the shapes one or two at a time. Staple around edge of shape about every two inches leaving a

7-16

small space for pushing in stuffing. (Figure 7-17.) Stuff each shape with used nylons. (They will be somewhat flat; yet three-dimensional.) Staple shut the small space left for stuffing.

2. *Cover the Papier-Maché Strips:*

Tear newspaper into thick strips about 2″ x 5″. Dip each strip into paste and put onto the shape in an overlapping design. Carefully overlap strips around the sides. (Figure 7-18.) Tear comic sections of newspapers into strips about 2″ x 5″. After both sides have been covered with a layer of black and white newspaper strips, cover with a layer of colored strips. Let dry thoroughly.

7-17

3. *Paint with Tempera paint in appropriate or desired colors.*

Specific Skills and Concepts To Be Learned:

1. Shapes can be stuffed.
2. They can be huge as well as small.
3. Fruits are composed of basic shapes: spheres, cones, cylinders.

7-18

Adaptations:

Older children may use these Fruit Shapes for dance decorations or for parties. To make them a bit more glamorous, try adding pieces of shiny paper, or decorate with glitter.

LESSON 6: SNOW TRANSFORMS SHAPES! CREATE SNOW SHAPES BY THINKING UP A STORM

Falling snow transforms a dirty world into a sparkling, crystalline fairyland. New shapes emerge as the snow covers and joins several shapes together. New shapes also can emerge from the hands and minds of creative children and teachers.

Tools, Materials and Equipment:

Blue construction paper	Water containers
Paint brushes	Newspaper

Tempera paint | Snow pictures
White chalk | Play shovels
Large wooden spoons | Wooden sticks

Preparation:

Think about snow and its many aspects. What are the colors of snow? Is it always white? How does the sky look before, after and during a snow storm? Where does snow stick? What happens when it melts? What shapes do you see when it is snowing or after a storm? What new ones emerge? Look at some snow pictures or Currier and Ives prints and discuss.

Developmental Procedure for Activity:

This lesson contains two activities, one for indoors and the other for outside.

1. *Snow Paintings:*

Make a snow picture on a sheet of blue paper, 12" x 18". It may be very simple, just sketching a snowman and lots of snowflakes, or it can be quite complex, with a landscape showing trees, housing, people, fences, etc. The complexity, of course, depends upon the age of the child making the picture. (Figure 7-19.) White chalk is excellent for sketching in the designs.

Develop the picture by painting in various colors, leaving some areas for the white tempera. Let dry thoroughly. (NOTE: FOR THE VERY YOUNG CHILD, just let him paint a snow picture, as he desires.) (Figure 7-20.)

7-19

7-20

7-21

Next, use the white paint to transform the shapes as the snow does when it falls. New shapes may be added, too. (Figure 7-21.)

2. *Snow Sculpture:*

After a snowstorm, teacher can discuss how shapes can be made in snow. This is called snow sculpture, and is made by building up a form with large or small snowballs, or by making piles of snow and, then, carving sections away. (Figure 7-22.)

Demonstrate the above procedures, substituting plasticene clay for the snow, working on a small scale. (Figure 7-23.) Stress that the sculptures should be simple, and not too realistic. (Realism is often hard and is unimportant to the young child.)

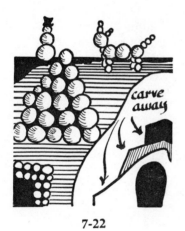

7-22

7-23

Now, go outdoors and make some real snow sculpture. Dress warmly. Wrap up! Play shovels, large wooden spoons, and pieces of wood (about 2″ x 1″ x 12″) are useful tools for packing snow and cutting away the shapes.

Specific Skills and Concepts To Be Learned:

1. Regular shapes can be transformed by snow.
2. Snow and clay are sculptural materials that can be used similarly.
3. Sculpture involves adding to and taking away materials.
4. Snow is not always white.

Adaptations:

Children can build imaginary snow sculptures using plasticene or ceramic clay. They can make snow people, architecture, and new shapes.

LESSON 7: CIRCULAR SHAPES IN CLAY!
SLAB TEPEES THAT SEND OUT SMOKE SIGNALS

The Plains Indians lived in tepees, decorated with symbols. In this lesson, children learn to make a tepee from ceramic clay.

Tools, Materials and Equipment:

Newspapers	Tempera paint
Ceramic clay	Small paint brushes
Old broom handles	Pencils
Water containers	Coffee can lids, small and large

Preparation:

Review the use of ceramic clay as described in Chapter Three, Lesson 3, "Animals Sound Different."

Cut old broom handles, or 1" dowel sticks into 10" lengths to be used for rolling clay.

Developmental Procedure for Activity:

1. Wedge Clay:

Give each child a lump of clay about the size of a large orange. Two children will share one roller.

If the clay is not new, and has been used before, wedge it to remove air bubbles. Place clay on the table and pound with roller. (Figure 7-24.) Air bubbles can cause a piece of ceramics to explode in the kiln.

7-24

2. Make a Base:

Roll slab of clay into a circular shape, as if making a pie. Make it about ½" thick. Now place small coffee can lid on top and trace around the edges with a sharp pencil point. This should cut the circle away from the rest of the clay. (Figure 7-25.)

Put name on the under side of the base, and using a bit of water on a finger, smooth the edges of the base.

3. *Make Sides:*

Roll a circular slab as in Number 2 above; place large coffee can lid on top, and cut a circle. Cut away half of the circle with the pencil. Cut out a triangle for the door. Cut a small half circle at side above door. (Figure 7-26.) Smooth all edges with wet finger. Twist the tepee sides into a cone shape. Moisten the back seams with water, rough up with fingernail and weld firmly together with fingers. (Figure 7-27.) Always join the parts SECURELY. Press together and press all around the joint.

Moisten base and lower edge of tepee and weld the two parts firmly together with fingers. (Figure 7-28.)

7-25

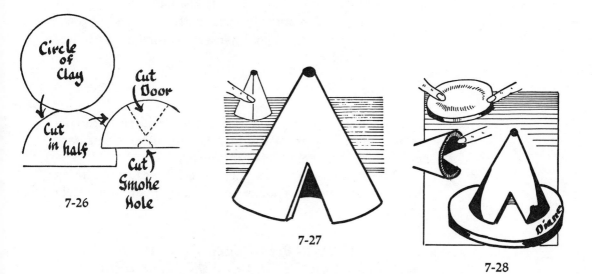

7-26

7-27

7-28

For the joining steps, the teacher may need to help the children who are having difficulty twisting and adhering sides to base.

If any cracks appear, moisten with fingertips dipped in water and rub away the crack. Allow to dry thoroughly, and fire in kiln, if one is available. Tepees will be harder, washable and less breakable, if fired.

7-29

4. *Paint Tepees:*

When dry, or after firing, draw designs on both the base and the sides. Outline the design in black, and paint in colors one at a time. (Do not paint inside tepee.) (Figure 7-29.)

Young children may paint in any way they wish. Grades two and three should be able to paint a design, and older children may make detailed designs.

When completed, a lighted cigarette can be placed inside the doorway (or perhaps a candle) and the smoke will emerge from the little hole at the top. THIS IS NOT MEANT TO ENDORSE CIGARETTE SMOKING AND THIS SHOULD BE MADE CLEAR TO CHILDREN.

Specific Skills and Concepts To Be Learned:

1. Ceramic clay must be wedged to remove air bubbles or sculpture may explode in the kiln.
2. Welding clay must be done with water and fingers.
3. Firing makes clay harder, washable and less breakable.

Adaptations:

This activity can be done by young children, although some will need help from the teacher. All other elementary school children will enjoy this experience.

Older children may glaze their tepees instead of painting with tempera. This, of course, then makes them completely washable.

LESSON 8: SQUEEZE A HEAD!
MAKING ACCIDENTAL CERAMIC CLAY HEADS

A blob of clay, squeezed with both hands and a little imagination creates a funny head. These sculptures have a lot of unusual expressions and somewhat resemble distorted rocks.

Tools, Materials and Equipment:

Newspapers	Ceramic clay
Tempera paint	Paint brushes
Water containers	

Preparation:

Review ceramic clay procedures, in the previous lesson and in Chapter Three, Lesson 3.

Developmental Procedure for Activity:

1. Give each child a large lump of clay, grapefruit size. Suggest that the clay be rolled into a cylinder shape.

2. Place both hands on cylinder shape and try to squeeze a form that will become a head and face. It's there; it just has to be SQUEEZED out. (Figure 7-30.) It's really not hard to do, but may require some strength in hands, *if clay is not soft and pliable.* If young children have difficulty, simply let them push and pull a face out of the clay a little at a time.

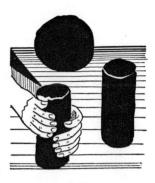

7-30

3. Now use a little imagination, and give the clay a little help . . . . then pull out a nose and push in some eyes and a mouth (if they are not already there). (Figure 7-31.)

Allow the children complete freedom to let any type of head form emerge, whether it be a monster, human, animal or purely an imaginative adventure. If they are not pleased with their initial results, suggest they keep trying and squeezing until a good accident happens.

Allow plenty of time to dry. Fire in a kiln if possible, and paint with tempera. If heads are very heavy, it will be necessary to hollow out some of the clay, or push a finger inside, to let the inner clay dry out. (Figure 7-32.) (If the piece is not thoroughly dried out, it may explode in the kiln.)

7-31

Specific Skills and Concepts To Be Learned:

1. Clay features on a face are both pulled out and pushed in.
2. Our hands and fingers are very useful tools when working with ceramics.
3. The use of one's imagination is very necessary in the creation of art.
4. Sculpture is inside the clay, just waiting to be squeezed out.

Adaptations:

This lesson can be used with children of all ages. However, older children will usually spend more time on the features,

7-32

their placement, details and textural effects. Younger children will arrive at a quick solution that will satisfy them, even if the teacher is not satisfied. However, each child's work is personal, and should NEVER BE CONDEMNED.

LESSON 9: COKE KITTENS ARE MORE THAN LUMPS OF CLAY! MAKE BOTTLE-SHAPED SCULPTURES

Kittens are especially appealing to children. They love to look at, cuddle and pat them. Why not make a pattable kitten that won't be hurt by a child's hands. Try one with a few simple shapes and molded from some ceramic clay.

Tools, Materials and Equipment:

Newspapers   Paint brushes
Ceramic clay   Water containers
Tempera paint

Preparation:

Continue the ceramic procedures as worked on previously.
Demonstrate the making of a cat from a few simple shapes: ball, bottle and coil.

Developmental Procedure for Activity:

1. Give each child two lumps of clay, one the size of a plum, and one the size of an orange.
2. Roll the smaller lump into a nice round ball. Pinch off a small amount from the bigger lump and make two very small pyramids. Adhere these to the top of the ball for the kitten's ears. (Figure 7-33.)
3. Pull out a small amount of clay for the cat's nose and mouth. (Figure 7-34.)
4. Roll and push the large ball into a bottle shape. Attach the head to the bottle body with fingers and water. (Figure 7-35.)
5. Give children an additional small amount of clay for a tail. Roll a thin coil, make it pointed at the end, and attach it at

7-33

7-34

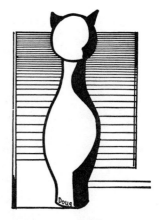

7-35

the BEGINNING and ENDING to the body. (It will be less breakable if securely attached in this way.) (Figure 7-36.)

6. Add legs, if desired; however, it's not really necessary since the shape already looks like a cat.

7. Let dry thoroughly, fire in kiln if possible and then paint with tempera.

NOTE: Some children may be unhappy making a cat. If so, allow them to make another animal from the ball, bottle and coil shapes.

Specific Skills and Concepts To Be Learned:

1. Simple shapes can be put together to create a new shape.
2. Keeping all parts attached in a piece of sculpture makes it stronger.

7-36

Adaptations:

This experience is of value for all grade levels. Older children may add paws, fur textures, and other special details. They also may wish to glaze the piece.

LESSON 10: DOUGH DUCKS FROM SALT AND FLOUR! BAKED DOUGH SCULPTURES

Substitute salt and flour clay for natural clay and then bake a bird in the oven . . . just like Thanksgiving Day!

Tools, Materials and Equipment:

Brushes	Oven
Varnish	Salt
Dry tempera paint	Warm water
Two large pots	Flour
Wire	Measuring cup

Preparation:

For a class of 24, the following recipe should provide enough clay for a small piece of sculpture, about 5", for each child.

Mix dough as follows:

1. Add two cups salt to three cups of warm water, stirring the salt into the water. Allow to cool.
2. Divide mixture into two equal parts.
3. Add ½ cup red dry tempera paint to one part and ½ cup blue to the other part.
4. Add 4 cups of flour to each part and knead each mixture for about ten minutes. Use at once.

Developmental Procedure for Activity:

Children will use this medium as they do ceramic and plasticene clay. It can be pinched, pulled, rolled, made textural, and easily manipulated even by the very young.

It is suggested that kindergarten children may use this clay to make birds, nests and eggs in their own way. Teacher should stress pushing parts together carefully so that they are joined and will not fall apart.

Primary children may make birds in the same way as the very young child does or they may make ducks as follows:

1. Roll an egg shape and flatten slightly. This is the body. (Figure 7-37a.)
2. Roll a short snake for a neck. Bend. Make a tapered bill and attach by pressing onto body. (Figure 7-37b.)
3. Make a very flat small egg, flatten it until it is quite thin, and press in place for a wing. (Figure 7-38a.)
4. Make a dot of dough for an eye and press on.

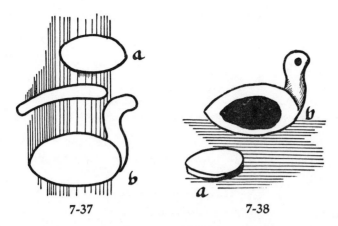

7-37   7-38

5. Be sure to use the two colors to contrast with each other, i.e., a red wing on a blue body, a red neck, a blue eye. (Figure 7-38b.)

6. Make a small loop of clay and place on the back. Insert a piece of wire in loop for hanging. (Figure 7-39.)

7-39

Bake at 300° F. for about one hour. After baking, give each piece a coat of varnish to make shiny, to protect the pieces, and help them survive for a long period of time.

Specific Skills and Concepts To Be Learned:

1. Salt and flour clay is easily manipulated.
2. It can be precolored with powdered tempera paint.

3. Varnish makes the salt and flour sculptures shiny, and protects the surface.

Adaptations:

This may be used with all age levels. In addition, the following experiences may be enjoyed:

1. Mix the recipe without the powdered paint. Bake and then paint with acrylics. More variations in color can be utilized in this way.

2. Use the recipe with no color; merely varnish the surface for an attractive golden brown finish.

3. Model different shapes.

4. Make ornaments for a Christmas tree.

5. Create jewelry.

6. Glaze with shellac instead of varnish.

8

Using Surface Textures

The human body responds to texture through both the tactile and visual senses. Texture helps us recognize objects and gives greater interest to everything we experience with touch and sight, adding dimension to our awareness.

Texture is the surface quality of an object or material. All objects have unique surfaces as a result of their basic structures. For example, the grain (or texture) of wood is different from the grain (or texture) of alabaster. Rabbit's fur looks and feels nothing like fish scales.

Textures can be compared: smooth vs. rough, dull vs. shiny. They can be modified by the application of a tool. (Sandpaper will smooth wood.) They can be changed by the addition of another material to the surface. (Varnishing wood makes it shiny.)

Textures can be symbolized with flat representation, as grass is represented by the drawing of lines. Then, too, textural representation can be imitative, as is done in palette knife painting. Thick paint is applied to give the illusion of the roundness of an orange and at the same time, creates a tactile effect.

Texture, then, as the subject of this chapter, can be enjoyed through lessons that will involve looking at enlarged minute surface qualities, drawing with crystals, painting on shiny surfaces, on rubbed and molded textures, and on synthetic and symbolic textures.

For additional activities dealing with textures, see Chapter Two, *Developing The Tactile Sense.*

LESSON 1: ENLARGE MINUTE SUBSTANCES! MAGNIFY A TEXTURE

How does the surface quality of a microcosm of our environment look . . . . . when enlarged? Explore this tiny world of textural surfaces.

Tools, Materials and Equipment:

Opaque projector	Magnifying glass
Microscope	Substances for viewing
	Crayons
	Newsprint

Preparation:

Collect various substances that are made up of tiny particles: table salt, epsom salts, pepper, sugar, seeds, spices and seasonings.

Developmental Procedure for Activity:

8-1

Look at each substance under a magnifying glass or microscope, or project onto a screen with an opaque projector. (Figure 8-1.)

Study and compare them. What do you think they resemble? (rocks, mountains, ants?) How DO they look when magnified? Does their textural appearance change under magnification?

Discussion and comparison of texture should give it meaning for the student and provide additional knowledge about his environment.

After looking at the various substances, suggest that students make drawings based on what they remember about the enlargements. Make this a simple drawing activity using newsprint and crayons.

Specific Skills and Concepts To Be Learned:

1. Suface qualities may be analyzed and compared.
2. Textures of substances are all different.
3. Tiny textures look quite different to the eye when they are magnified.

Adaptations:

Explore other textures and discuss their relative similarities and differences. Compare the textural qualities of animals, plants, rocks and earth.

LESSON 2: DRAW WITH CRYSTALS! USING SALT AS A TEXTURAL EXPERIENCE

Table salt, a colorless, crystalline solid, is used for seasoning or preserving food. Can you draw with it? . . . Or draw into it?

Tools, Materials and Equipment:

Table salt	Dry tempera paint
Flat box or shallow cake pan	

Preparation:

Collect materials and prepare as follows:

1. Place about ¼″ deep layer of table salt in a flat box or shallow cake pan.

2. Mix in a little dry tempera paint, using bright colors, such as red or blue. (Figure 8-2.)

3. Mix salt and paint together carefully.

NOTE: One box for two or three children will be sufficient, with each child having a turn to draw.

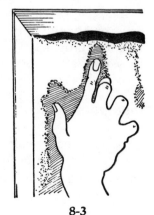

8-2   8-3

Developmental Procedure for Activity:

Children can get acquainted with a textural feeling-sensation by drawing pictures or designs in the colored salt, using fingers and hands. (Figure 8-3.) When finished, shake the box gently, and presto . . . magic . . ., the picture will disappear and a new drawing can be made.

Specific Skills and Concepts To Be Learned:

1. Salt can be colored.
2. Fingers and hands can draw in salt.
3. Salt is a textural medium.

Adaptations:

Experiment with sand or flour in this same way. Can you draw into it?

LESSON 3: PAINTING ON SHINY SURFACES! EXPLORE THE QUALITIES OF METALLIC PAPER

Eyes will open WIDE, when your children see shiny paper. Hold it under chins and notice the reflections! While it is usually used as a cut paper activity, it makes an exciting background for a painting.

Tools, Materials and Equipment:

Metallic paper 9" x 12" or Aluminum foil	Tempera paint Juice cans
Paint brushes	Newspapers
Water containers	Liquid soap (or detergent)

Preparation:

Metallic paper comes in several colors with white paper on the back. All are fun to use as a painting surface. (If metallic paper is too expensive, aluminum foil works well, too.)

Pour tempera into juice cans. Add a few drops of liquid soap (or detergent) to insure that paint will adhere to the smooth surface. Mix well. (Figure 8-4.) Prepare one set of red, yellow, and blue, plus black and white paint for every four children.

8-4

8-5

Developmental Procedure for Activity:

1. Allow children to select a sheet of shiny paper in the color they like.

2. Analyze the texture: Note how light reflects from the paper's surface. Feel it! What words can be used to describe it's texture: smooth, slippery, glossy, shiny, cold?

3. What other glossy surfaces have you seen? Where?

4. Make a painting on the metallic background using one of these topics: "My Favorite Design," "Lines and Colors I Like," "Interesting Shapes," "Kites and Balloons." (Figure 8-5.)

5. When finished, there should be glints of metallic paper between the paint strokes. This gives a fascinating appearance to the child's painting.

Specific Skills and Concepts To Be Learned:

1. Metallic paper comes in various colors.
2. It has a smooth, shiny surface, which reflects light.
3. Tempera paint will not stick to a shiny surface unless soap or detergent is added to the paint.

Adaptations:

This lesson should be used only after children have had several painting experiences and have learned how (a) to control the drippiness of paint and (b) to use several colors without getting a muddy mixture. Therefore it can be used at the end of the kindergarten year and for all the children in grades one through eight.

Further experiments may be carried out as follows:

1. Paint metallic paper with a solid coat of black tempera. Scratch a picture through the painted surface only. Use a scissors' blade or sharpened dowel stick for making the scratchboard.

3. Collect used greeting cards made with foil. Paint miniature pictures on the foil.

LESSON 4: SYNTHETIC TEXTURES! PALETTE KNIFE PAINTING WITH TONGUE DEPRESSORS

A synthetic texture is one where a surface is changed with a tool to produce a surface quality that imitates another surface quality.

Tools, Materials and Equipment:

Finger paint, moist	Paper towels
Tongue depressors	Plastic egg cartons
Van Gogh reproductions	Small containers
Spoons	Cardboard 6" x 8"
Water containers	(or larger)

Preparation:

Prepare Paint:

One eggbox is required for each two children. Place two teaspoons of red, yellow, blue, green, black and white finger paint in egg cartons. (If moist finger paint is unavailable, mix a little school paste with powdered tempera paint.)

Plastic egg cartons are very convenient in the classroom since:

1. The cover can be used to mix colors as desired.

2. They are convenient holders for saving paint to be used another day. Paints will stay moist.

Look at reproductions of the paintings of Vincent Van Gogh.

Discuss how he used thick paint that not only was textural but seemed to make objects move. His trees had textural bark and, at the same time, seemed to be growing right out of the painting. He painted textural stars that seemed to be whirling around in a textural sky.

Demonstrate

Show how to make a palette knife painting using either a special knife or a tongue depressor (or both). Show the texture of the objects with the paint. (Figure 8-6.)

8-6

Developmental Procedure for Activity:

1. Use a tongue depressor to mix colors and apply paint to the cardboard surface. Use PLENTY of paint. (Colors can be mixed right on the newspaper covering the table top.)

2. Whenever new colors are desired, clean tongue depressor by dipping into water container and wipe off on a paper towel.

3. Create interesting shapes and textures with the finger paint. Don't be concerned with reality, since it could be too difficult for young children.

Older children can use themes of "Leaves," "Flowers," or "Still Life" but nonrealism presents less pressure to come up with something that looks good. Instead, young children can devote their thoughts to looking at the textures, applying the paint, and keeping colors bright and beautiful.

Specific Skills and Concepts To Be Learned:

1. Vincent Van Gogh made textural paintings.
2. Palette knife and tongue depressor paintings are textural.
3. It is possible to make textures on cardboard.
4. Textures can be simulated with paint.

Adaptations:

1. Use little blocks of cloth, wadded up, to dab paint onto a surface. Let dry. Spray a bit of silver or gold on the dry paint.

2. Cut down (to shorten) a toothbrush. Use it to apply the paint in swirls, zigzags, multiple lines. (Figure 8-7.)

3. Apply paint with a hair roller, pipe cleaner or a stiff bristled brush.

4. Make a palette knife painting and sprinkle with silver glitter while wet.

8-7

LESSON 5: TEXTURE BY RUBBING!
MAKE CRAYON RUBBINGS OF REAL SURFACES

Take the children for a walk around the school, in and outside, and make rubbings of actual textures.

Tools, Materials and Equipment:

Crayons	Newspaper
Masking tape	Juice cans
Brushes	Newsprint or typing paper,
Thin tempera paint	white and/or colored

Preparation:

Thin tempera by adding ¾ cup water to ¼ cup liquid paint. Mix well. Three each of red, green and blue will be sufficient for the entire class. They can easily share colors.

Developmental Procedure for Activity:

Demonstrate rubbing technique as follows:

1. Place a piece of newsprint over an object, such as a brick, or small tiles.

2. If a young child is doing this, have him tape his paper over the object to keep if from slipping. (Figure 8-8.)

3. Use the side of a large peeled crayon. Hold it flat against the paper and go over the object. (Figure 8-9.)

4. Continue to rub over the top of the object, pressing

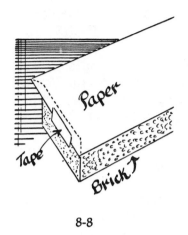

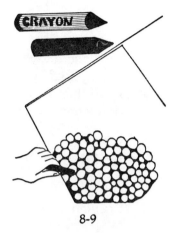

8-8   8-9

firmly and evenly until the object's texture has completely emerged.

Now walk around the school, inside and/or outside, trying to make as many textures as you can find: wire mesh, metal, plaster, leaves, cloth, bricks, tile, or any textural surface.

Make rubbings . . . look at real textures . . . feel textures . . . discuss how they look.

Return to the classroom and go over the rubbings with thinned paint. If they are really strong, with plenty of wax crayon on the paper surface, the paint should run off the textures, filling in the space between them. (Figure 8-10.)

8-10

Specific Skills and Concepts To Be Learned:

1. Crayon rubbing over an object's surface shows its actual texture.
2. Looking at real objects helps one understand the surface texture of an object.
3. Paint, when thinned, runs off a wax surface.

Adaptations:

Look carefully at, and collect leaves and grasses. Then . . .

1. Arrange on a flat surface.
2. Tape a piece of paper over the grasses.
3. Make a rubbing of the arrangement.

LESSON 6: SYMBOLIC TEXTURES!
MAKE CRAYON DRAWINGS OF SURFACES

Symbolic drawing helps in the recognition of objects. A dog is recognized by the lines drawn to show his fur. Short, vertical green lines represent grass while slashing vertical lines all over a drawing are symbols of rain.

Tools, Materials and Equipment:

Crayons	Newsprint
Drawing paper	Newspapers
Magazines	

Preparation:

Search for examples of textural drawings in newspapers and magazines. Cut out and place on the bulletin board and discuss the various symbolic textures. What are the textures for bricks, wood, bark, leaves, fur, sand, clouds?

Developmental Procedure for Activity:

Continue looking for textural drawings. See juvenile picture books for fine examples: animals in grass, birds with feathers, children with flowing hair.

Draw pictures of textures. Draw from a real model such as a calm cat, rabbit, hamster, or dog. (GENTLY. . .FEEL THE TEXTURES OF THE ANIMAL.)

Specific Skills and Concepts To Be Learned:

1. Symbolic drawing helps in the recognition of objects.
2. Textural drawings can be found in books, magazines and newspapers.
3. With a real model, you can feel texture.

Adaptations:

Upper grade children may also draw with pencils, pens, crayons, chalk, to create symbolic textures. They, too, may draw from the model and, in addition, may carry out the procedure into scratchboard and even linoleum block prints.

Stuffed animals may be substituted for the real models (for young children.) Especially use those made with soft, furry or scratchy fur.

LESSON 7: MOLDING TEXTURES!
MAKE A TEXTURED CERAMIC TILE

Textured tiles make interesting wall plaques. They can also be used in quantity to make a mural.

Tools, Materials and Equipment:

Ceramic clay	Newspaper
Kiln	Water containers
Tools for texturing	Rolling pins or dowels
Tempera paint, stain or glaze	Plastic bags

Preparation:

Collect tools that can be used for texturing: old tooth brushes, dull knives, forks, sponges, spoons, burlap, screening, combs, pencils, old compasses.

Developmental Procedure for Activity:

8-11

Cover tables with newspaper and give each child a ball of ceramic clay, about the size of an orange. Roll the clay into a pancake about ½" thick. Dip a finger into water and smooth out all the cracks, and the edges. Now cut the pancake into an interesting shape: square, rectangular, circular, or even a peanut shape (free form). (Figure 8-11.)

Again smooth edges and cracks on top or under side. Let dry overnight or until leathery.

Now use the texturing tools and create a picture or a design. Wet a toothbrush and go over a section with the stiff bristles. (Figure 8-12.) Scratch designs or pictures, or even lines into the surface with a knife. (Figure 8-13.) Make multiple

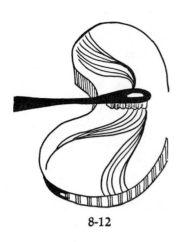

8-12

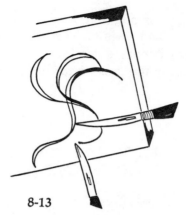

8-13

8-14

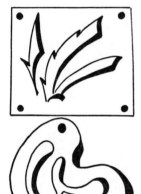

8-15

designs with a fork's tines. Use an old compass point to draw into the clay. Use a spoon to depress the clay, pressing down hard. Use a straw to make tiny circles. (Figure 8-14.)

Turn tile over, and put child's name on the under side. Use a pointed object to make holes in the tile, one at each corner. (Figure 8-15.) Place a plastic bag and a heavy book on top of each plaque to prevent warping. Allow to dry. (Takes from three days to a week.)

When dry, fire in kiln, after which glaze can be applied. (If desired, stain or tempera paint may be used.) Glazed tiles, of course, will require refiring.

Specific Skills and Concepts To Be Learned:

1. Designs may be incised into clay tiles.
2. Various tools may be used to create textural effects.
3. The textures shown on a tile will be the direct result of the tool's structure and shape.
4. Clay tiles warp. To avoid this, they must be weighted down during the drying process.

Adaptations:

It is preferable for young children to make free-form shapes; ones that do not have to be precisely measured. Work on the tile may be performed while it is still rather moist instead of leather-hard.

Also, it is not recommended that they wait for two firings in a kiln. They always want to take it HOME RIGHT NOW, and to them, waiting is *tragic*. Nevertheless, the tiles are stronger if they are fired. It is , therefore, recommended that they be placed in a kiln one time only and then painted with tempera.

9

Utilization of Space

We exist in space and there is space within us. We have space in our stomach when we are hungry, space for air in our lungs, space for blood in our veins. Space is basic to life as it is to art.

In sculpture, painting and architecture, space is created, simulated and enclosed. The painter and the sculptor simulate space by making a flat surface appear to have depth. They attempt to create a new reality, based on the world of fact. They make forms and space work together, for one cannot exist without the other. All artists work with open and enclosed spaces as they design architectural structures, sculptures and paintings.

To the young child, the mention of the word "space" brings visions of rockets and life in outer space. He has his own ideas of space. Also, while he can recognize the near and far in pictures; in his art, he uses space according to his stage of development. For example, the very young child scribbles all over his paper, and gradually, as he grows and develops, his work has structure, more control, and his use of space changes. He may line his objects up at the bottom. Later the ground is placed at the bottom of the painting and the sky is shown way up at the top. As he grows older, the child usually learns to overlap shapes and use perspective. For these reasons, it is suggested that children continue having numerous experiences in drawing and painting.

This chapter, of course, is presented as a means of furthering the child's spatial development. In it are presented opportunities for working with the utilization of space in a variety of ways: on paper, in boxes, in sculpture, moving in the air, and other simple techniques.

LESSON 1: FILLING SPACE!
MAKING FELT MARKER SPACE DOODLES

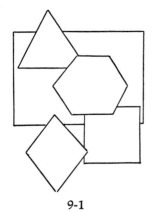

In this lesson, the children fill in space on geometrically shaped oaktag.

Tools, Materials and Equipment:

Oaktag	Felt markers
Scissors	Cord
Paper punch	

Preparation:

9-1

Introduce the activity by letting the children have fun doodling on the chalkboard. (They LOVE IT.) Give all a chance to participate, filling the entire space.

For young children, precut geometrical shapes from oaktag (about 6″ in length or diameter). Older children may cut their own. (Figure 9-1.)

Developmental Procedure for Activity:

Fill the shapes by drawing more geometrical shapes and lines with felt-tipped markers. Try the following:

9-2

1. Dots, circles, big and little, all over the shape.
2. Lines, thick and thin
3. Curved lines.
4. Lightening lines
5. Combine circles and lines.

Invent your own designs, being certain to fill all the empty space. Be IMAGINATIVE! For example, fill in design with oval shapes. Every other one is white and every other one is black. The white one has black dots in it and the black one has white dots. (Figure 9-2.)

Fill the other side of each shape, too, with doodle designs, so that when they are hung up, the shapes will be attractive when seen from any angle.

Punch holes in them and slip string through the holes as shown in Figure 9-3. Hang all your pieces together on one cord.

9-3

Specific Skills and Concepts To Be Learned:

1. Spaces on paper can be empty or filled.
2. Designs should be made on both sides of a shape if it is to be hung up for decorative purposes.
3. Shapes can be connected with string.

Adaptations:

Older children may make drawings or designs to fit the space of the particular geometrical shape used.

LESSON 2: PINPRICKING!
PUNCH A HOLE DESIGN IN PAPER

In England and Colonial America, pinprick decoration was quite popular with pictures of people, flowers and landscapes made by piercing paper with a needle. The designs were often used in the making of lamp shades.

These artists were, in effect, creating miniature areas of negative space. In this lesson, too, space is made through puncturing.

Tools, Materials and Equipment:

Typing paper	White glue
Needles, pins, corsage pins, nails	
Scissors	Metallic paper
Masking tape	Boxes
Paper punch	Dark construction paper
Tissue	Poster board

Preparation:

New space can be made within space. A piece of paper with nothing on it contains space, and if we puncture it to make holes, we can create new space.

Demonstrate! Cut a hole in a piece of paper. Hold it up to show the class that there is space where the hole is, and space around the hole where the paper is. The hole area is called NEGATIVE SPACE; the paper area is called POSITIVE

SPACE. The space occupied by the paper is the positive space. It encloses, and outlines the void or negative space. (THIS IS NOT APPROPRIATE FOR THE VERY YOUNG CHILD but the upper primary child should be able to understand it.) The negative or void space is empty.

Now how can we make more negative spaces in this paper? Cut with scissors? Paper punch . . . awl . . . punch out with a pencil, pin, nail, needle?

Let's make some positive-negative space designs. (When talking to the very young child, simply state that we are going to make some hole designs.)

Developmental Procedure for Activity:

1. Securely tape a piece of typing paper to a box (whose size is smaller than the paper). Fold paper over at the corners and double tape if necessary, for real tautness. (Figure 9-4.)

2. Using a needle, nail or pin, punch holes to make a picture or design. (Figure 9-5.)

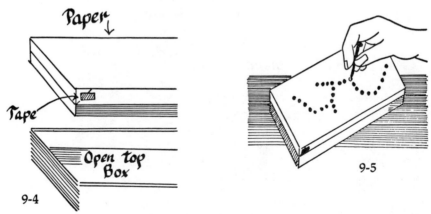

9-4

9-5

3. When completed, take tape off carefully. Turn paper over. The side that has a raised pinprick surface is the side that should be kept on top.

4. Trim off any rough edges.

5. Mount on any dark-colored construction paper.

Specific Skills and Concepts To Be Learned:

1. Pinprick decoration was popular in England and Colonial America.

2. A hole is negative space and it is surrounded by positive space.

3. Designs and pictures can be made by making holes (or negative space) in paper.

Adaptations:

Older children can punch holes (with nails and a hammer) in tin cans. A candle can be inserted and the light will show up through the holes. (Figure 9-6.)

Other adaptations are shown below:

9-6

1. Use same process as shown under "Developmental Procedures For Activity" but substitute metallic paper for typing paper. Shiny side should be the underside when working on it; top side when completed. Glue colored paper on back. Display by taping to windows, and note how the light will come through the negative space.

2. Use small, long rectangular pieces of colored poster board. Punch holes with a paper punch, (makes a larger negative space.) Display on windows. (Figure 9-7.)

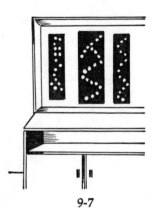

LESSON 3: EXPANDING SHAPES IN SPACE! CUT OUT SOME SIMPLE PAPER MOBILES

9-7

Paper has great possibilities for use in space, especially when it's cut in such a way that it can be expanded and hung to gently sway in the breeze.

Tools, Materials and Equipment:

Scissors   Paste
String   Construction paper

Preparation:

Expand paper by working with the following activities:

1. *Expandable Circles:* (Or Squares)
Cut a circle and then make a long continuous cut until you reach the center. The same process can be used with a square. (See Figure 9-8.)

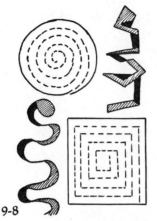

9-8

9-9

2. *Expandable Cylinder:*

Fold a rectangular piece of paper back and forth, as for a fan. Then curve it around so that the two ends come together. Paste. (See Figure 9-9.)

3. *Expandable Fringe:*

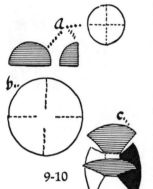

9-10

Cut a circle. Fold in half, and in half again. . . and again. (Figure 9-10a.) Open up and cut towards the center, on every folded line. Stop cutting about one inch from the center. (Figure 9-10b.) Now fold up every other strip and fold down the in-between strip. (Figure 9-10c.)

4. *Expandable Ladder:*

Fold a rectangular piece of paper in half, and in half again. (Figure 9-11a.) Cut slashes on one side and then in between the first slashes, but on the opposite side. (Figure 9-11b.)

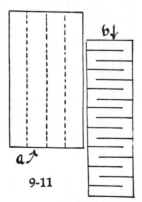

9-11

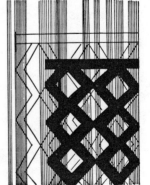

9-12

Open up and pull apart gently. (Figure 9-12.)

5. *Expandable Pineapple:*

Make a circle. Fold it in half, and in half again. Cut slashes in one side and then IN BETWEEN on the other side. (Figure 9-13a.) Gently pull open. (Figure 9-13b.)

6. *Expandable Lantern:*

Fold a rectangular piece of paper in half. Cut fringe on the folded side. (Figure 9-14a.) Open up and glue left to right side together. (Figure 9-14b.) Make four lantern shapes and glue together. (Figure 9-15.) Mobiles are designs that move in space. To make these paper expandables into simple mobiles that young children can put together, attach string to one or more of the paper shapes and hang so that the air will move them around. (Figure 9-16.)

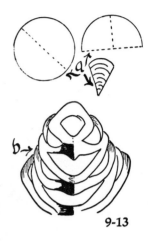

9-13

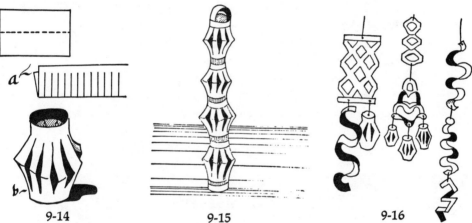

9-14   9-15   9-16

Specific Skills and Concepts To Be Learned:

1. Paper can be expanded by cutting and pulling.
2. Mobiles are designs that move in space.
3. The air causes them to move about.
4. Paper expandables can be combined to make simple mobiles.

Adaptations:

These ideas may be adapted for older children by having them cut cardboard into expandables using X-Acto knives or single-edged razor blades.

LESSON 4: SPATIAL WEAVING!
WEAVE A DESIGN IN A BOX

This lesson presents a very simple weaving activity.

Tools, Materials and Equipment:

Awl or paper punch	Box tops
Scissors	Masking tape
Colored cord: black and red	

Preparation:

For very young children, the teacher must prepare the following materials in advance of the lesson:

1. Cut out the top of a box, with strong scissors or a razor blade, leaving an inch border around the edge. (Figure 9-17.)
2. Punch holes around edges, using an awl or strong paper punch. (Figure 9-18.)
3. Cut cord into 16" lengths.
4. Twist a 1" piece of masking tape around one end, making it into a point. This end will be used to weave with. The tape stiffens the cord and takes the place of a needle. (Figure 9-19a.)
5. Knot the other end of the cord. (Figure 9-19b.)

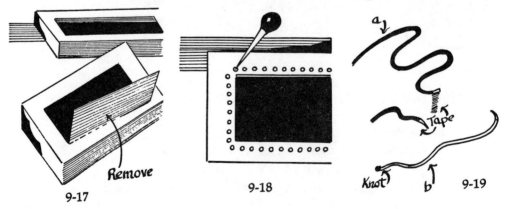

9-17   Remove   9-18   Knot   b   9-19

Developmental Procedure for Activity:

Weave a design in the box as follows:

1. Insert the taped end of the cord into a hole inside the box on the right hand side.

2. Pull the cord through, letting the knot stay inside the box. (Figure 9-20.)

3. Cross over the box, to the left side and slide taped cord through another hole.

4. Keep weaving back and forth from one side to the other until the cord is used up, at which time, a piece of tape can be placed over the end of the cord on the inside of the box. Older children can secure the end by knotting.

5. Start another colored cord and continue weaving. Then use another cord; and another, until the design is interesting to look at.

6. Holes at top and bottom are woven in the same manner as from left to right and right to left. (Figure 9-21.)

7. All space does not have to be filled in, since open spaces can contribute to an interesting design.

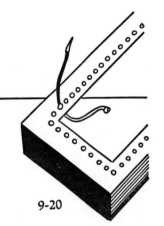

9-20

Specific Skills and Concepts To Be Learned:

1. A box can be used to make a woven design.
2. Weaving cord back and forth in a box fills in the open space.
3. The use of the bright and dark colors creates an interesting effect.

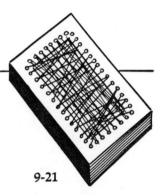

9-21

Adaptations:

This weaving process can also be done with:

1. A piece of styrofoam, with the center removed.
2. A picture frame with nails inserted around edge.

LESSON 5: SPACE ON STAGE!
CONVERT SHOE BOXES INTO DIORAMAS

Dioramas are actually small stages in which scenery, stage properties, tiny people and animals are placed. They are an excellent device for developing student skills in construction and working within contained space.

Tools, Materials and Equipment:

Shoe boxes	Plasticene clay
Crayons	Cotton

Felt markers	White glue
Scissors	Scrap box of paper
Small twigs	Blue tempera paint
Newspapers	Paint brushes
Water containers	Manila paper
Small boxes	Toothpicks
Straight pins	

Preparation:

Begin collecting!

1. Shoe boxes will be required. One per child!

2. Scrap materials can be placed in separate boxes. Sort these as they are brought in.

Developmental Procedure for Activity:

Spend a period discussing the subject of a snowstorm. What happens? What do you see? Who would be out in it? (Refer back to Chapter Seven, Lesson 6: "Snow Transforms Shapes," if desired.)

Now do a drawing of a snowstorm to reinforce the thoughts brought out. Use crayons on manila paper.

Actual work on dioramas may now commence:

Cotton Clouds

9-22

1. Paint the inside of the box a solid blue all around the sides and top, not the bottom. Let dry. Glue some cotton clouds here and there. (Figure 9-22.) Outside of box may also be painted, if desired.

2. What characters do we need in our diorama? What positions will they assume? Are they standing, sitting, kneeling, falling? How big should they be? (About 3" to 4" is rather effective.)

3. Draw the characters and color in with felt markers or crayons. Cut out. Some animals or people may be made with plasticene, if desired. Insert each figure in a plasticene blob, so that they are all free-standing. (Figure 9-23.)

4. What stage properties are needed for a snow scene? Make these also by drawing, coloring in and cutting out, OR:
. . .Put tiny twigs in blobs of clay for trees or bushes. Glue tiny bits of cotton on twigs. Put a little cotton on clay bases around the twigs.

9-23   9-24

. . .Make little box houses, color with crayons or markers and glue cotton on roof.

. . .Cover bottom of box with cotton. Glue down.

. . .Make a toothpick fence. (Stick into clay and place in snow.)

5. Place all objects, animals and people on top of the cotton snow. Secure in place by gluing or pushing pins in clay blobs. Arrange each so that it looks good and can be seen adequately. Stress that on the stage there is a background and a foreground. (Figure 9-24.)

Specific Skills and Concepts To Be Learned:

1. Dioramas are little stages.
2. A stage has a background and foreground.
3. Dioramas are made on a specific theme or subject.
4. Part of a diorama is flat (two-dimensional) and part stands out (three-dimensional).

Adaptations:

Older children may make more complex dioramas on any theme they select, making three-dimensional stage properties, animals and people.

Try illustrating a story with a diorama or do a stage set for a well-known play. Try Shakespeare.

LESSON 6: WORKING IN SPACE!
MAKE TOOTHPICK SCULPTURES

Toothpicks can be glued together to form a three-dimensional mass that has interesting internal space relationships. They can, also, be put together with other materials, as will be shown in this lesson.

Tools, Materials and Equipment:

Toothpicks	Old scissors
White glue	Cardboard bases
Dried whole peas	Small marshmallows
Clay	

Preparation:

In this lesson, we shall be building with toothpicks. Some will be lying down (horizontals) and some will be standing up (verticals). Put together, they will become three-dimensional constructions that have height, width and depth.

Buildings and sculptures can be made with toothpicks. We can design people, animals, bridges, and even trees. The toothpicks can be broken into different sizes. We can make a space construction to stand on a base or to swing from the ceiling. We can build pyramids, cubes and other shapes.

The lesson, then, should begin with a demonstration of the making of simple three-dimensional forms. Begin by punching holes into a cardboard base; put a small amount of glue into each hole, and push in a toothpick. (Any of the procedures described on the following pages may also be demonstrated.)

Developmental Procedure for Activity:

Toothpick construction for older children should begin with a possible plan of approach. What are they going to make? How will they do it?

Very young children can learn as they go along. Let them experiment! Give them the freedom to explore the medium, discovering the possibilities and limitations. WORKING WITH TOOTHPICKS IS REALLY A FINE PROJECT FOR DEVELOPING ONE'S SENSE OF SPATIAL RELATIONS.

Try the following construction ideas. See what will work best for your students:

1. *Toothpick-Clay Constructions:*

Roll clay into small lumps that can be used to hold the toothpicks together. If you use plasticene clay, after the experience is over, the materials can be taken apart and used for some other experience. HOWEVER, IT'S NOT EASY TO TAKE THEM AWAY FROM A YOUNG CHILD! They make you feel like SCROOGE!

For this kind of construction, simply push a toothpick into a blob of clay. Put another blob of clay on the other end. Push a toothpick into the blob and start building.

This procedure is quite conducive to creating cubes and thus simple architecture can be made. (Figure 9-25.)

2. *Toothpick-Marshmallow Constructions:*

Substitute a tiny marshmallow for a tiny blob of clay and start building.

3. *Toothpick-Pea Constructions:*

Prepare whole dried peas by soaking in water overnight, BUT NOT MORE THAN 24 HOURS.

Use the peas in the same manner as the above two experiences with clay and marshmallows.

When peas dry, they tend to shrink. If so, some of the toothpicks may loosen and will require a drop of glue placed on the loose joint.

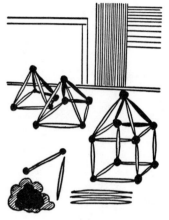

9-25

4. *Toothpick-Glue Constructions:*

Using a cardboard base, poke holes in the cardboard with an old scissors' point, place a drop of white glue in the hole, and press in a toothpick.

Make another hole, place glue in hole, press in a toothpick and let it lean against the first toothpick. Place a drop of glue where the two sticks meet. Continue in this manner, creating a structure. There will be empty spaces between the sticks but these make the design more interesting.

After the sculpture seems to be completed, and for that matter, during its creation, keep turning it around to see that it is exciting from all sides. The design will have many open or negative spaces which may or may not be interesting. If it is

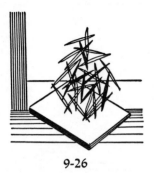

9-26

uninteresting, ask: "What can I do to make it better?" Then adjust it by adding more sticks, or a stick going in a different direction. (Figure 9-26.)

Another problem children may have is with the concept of BALANCE. If the construction gets too high, it may fall over. If it is too heavy on top, it will collapse. Balancing, too, will be a learning experience for the child as he works. However, the teacher must be on hand whenever this problem occurs to keep him from becoming discouraged.

After the toothpick sculpture has been completed, and if it is to be a permanent piece, spray it with fluorescent or gold paint, or paint with tempera.

NOTE: This last type of construction is by far the most difficult, and therefore, is not recommended for the very young child.

Specific Skills and Concepts To Be Learned:

1. Toothpicks can be used to create a three-dimensional design.
2. This design will have many open or negative spaces which may or may not be interesting.
3. Turning the design around helps one see spaces that are boring and which can be adjusted to make a more exciting sculptural piece.
4. Toothpicks can be held together by using glue, clay, candy, and even whole dried peas that have been soaked in water.

Adaptations:

Older children may build very large, complicated structures. Models of buildings can be made. Toothpicks may be cut into smaller sections using a sharp knife or razor blade. Tiny pieces of the sticks may be used to create:

1. Mini-miniatures
2. Tiny sculptures
3. Tiny buildings
4. Buildings with windows, doors, chimneys, etc.

10

Using Color

Color helps us *identify* and name objects. It *appeals* to our eyes and emotions, making us happy, sad, peaceful and even excited. We choose the colors we like to wear and to live with, for color gives *meaning* to our experiences. Color, also, tells us the *quality* of an object, i.e., whether a piece of fruit is ripe or if it has gone bad. We use colors for *messages.* Green means "go" and red means "stop." We can *compare* objects by color.

The source of color is light. When there is no light present, we cannot see color. Go into a dark room at night, and note that until a light has been turned on, no color can be seen.

An introduction to color should be simple for the young child, allowing his color knowledge to develop in an incidental way. He learns to use color in its simplest forms and, as he becomes aware, he'll be anxious to use it in all its intricacy. Formal teaching of color will confuse the young child. He usually wants to work with the brightest colors in the way he desires at the particular moment, or he may not care what color he is using, often painting a purple tree or a red picture of his mother.

As he grows older, and progresses through the primary grades, more difficult color problems may be introduced. For these reasons, this chapter will introduce the child to color, show how colors can be mixed, explored, changed; how colors are transparent, translucent, and opaque; how colors seem warm and cool. It will present lessons using paint, crayons, paper, and ink all with emphasis on seeing and knowing about COLOR.

LESSON 1: SOLID COLOR PICTURES!
ONE-COLOR DESIGNS FROM MAGAZINES

In this lesson, single colors are used for more learning experiences.

Tools, Materials and Equipment:

Books	Construction paper
Magazines	Collage materials
Scissors	Shoe boxes
Paste	Colored projects

Preparation:

Learn more about color by:

1. Reading or talking about stories in books and fairy tales that deal with color. (Examples: *Little Red Riding Hood; Goldilocks.*)

2. Talking about favorite colors? Why are they your favorites?

3. Do you select objects for their colors? Why?

4. Many objects have more than one color. A cat may be white, black and brown. Can you name some other objects that are multi-colored? (leaves, clothes, flowers, cars, toys.)

5. There are objects which come in different colors. For example, you may buy a box of facial tissues in green, yellow or pink. Lollypops come in red, yellow, and green. Can you name other objects like this?

Set up color boxes around the room.

1. Fill a shoe box with objects that are blue. Another with red objects; one with yellow; one with green; then orange and purple. Figure 10-1.

2. Let children explore the articles and discuss their findings with the class.

10-1

Developmental Procedure for Activity:

Give each pupil an old magazine. Have him select a color to work with. If the child selects red, then he will cut out all the red pieces he can find. Then, when he has finished, have him trade his magazine with another child and look for more red.

Give each pupil one piece of construction paper in the same color as the pieces he has cut from the magazines, i.e., if there are red pieces, then red construction paper is to be used. Arrange and paste the cut paper pieces in a design on the construction paper background. The result will be a one-color or monochromatic design.

When all are finished, tack up the completed work on the bulletin board. Compare and note the great variety of shades (dark tones) and tints (light tones) of each color.

Specific Skills and Concepts To Be Learned:

1. Many objects have the same color.
2. Some objects have more than one color within the object itself.
3. Some objects come in different colors.
4. There is a great variety of shades and tints of each color.

Adaptations:

Older students can utilize this lesson by adding other kinds of material IN THE SAME COLOR to make a collage. For a yellow collage, use yellow construction paper background, yellow scraps from magazines, yellow yarn, yellow cloth, yellow seeds, and other yellow items.

LESSON 2: COLORS, COLORS, COLORS! LEARNING TO SEE COLOR

This lesson introduces color as seen in nature.

Tools, Materials and Equipment:

Pictures or real objects for color study

Hard candies	Tempera paint
Newsprint	Paint brushes
Newspaper	Manila paper
Crayons	Juice cans for paint

Preparation:

Get acquainted with color by looking at nature. Talk about colors you see in flowers, insects, fruits, animals, and plants. We use color to identify and qualify objects. We know an orange is an orange, partly because it is orange in color. A green apple may not be ripe but a brown banana is overripe.

Offer each child a colored candy, allowing him to select the one he wants but asking why it is being selected. He may say, "I like the color," but undoubtedly he will reply, "I like the lemon flavor of yellow candy," or "the lime flavor of green." Point out that he is using color to identify an object.

Discuss the other ways that color tells us about an object. Red skin may be sunburned. A white face suggests illness. A black cookie suggests a burnt cookie.

Developmental Procedure for Activity:

Draw some objects that can be identified by color (such as those described previously). Draw these in a large size, with crayons. (Figure 10-2.)

10-2

Specific Skills and Concepts To Be Learned:

1. Color helps us identify and qualify objects.
2. Color tells us many things about an object.

Adaptations:

If the child is too young or is not ready for the use of natural color, simply allow him to do it HIS WAY.

Older children can work with this lesson by:

1. Painting still-life arrangements of fruit in various stages of ripeness.
2. Making collages of cut paper or magazine cutouts on people with different colors of skin or flowers of all colors.

LESSON 3: COLOR IN NATURE!
PAINTING LEAVES

Trace around real leaves and then make leaf paintings that are bright and COLORFUL!

Tools, Materials and Equipment:

Real leaves	Paint brushes
Chalk	Manila paper
Tempera paint	Water containers
Newspapers	Black felt-tipped markers

Preparation:

This lesson should be used after preliminary painting exercises have taken place, so the child knows how to clean a brush, how to keep colors pure, etc. This is described in Chapter One, *Lesson 1: Cover It With Paint.*

Continue discussions of color in nature, as begun in the previous lesson. Look at autumn leaves. Name the colors that can be seen in them.

Developmental Procedure for Activity:

Place a leaf on the manila paper. Using a piece of colored chalk, draw around the leaf. Move leaf and draw around it again. Keep moving leaf and redrawing for about five or six times. Then paint in the leaves, using bright, autumn colors. The colors, however, do not have to be realistic or copied from nature. (Figure 10-3.) Remember that young children usually will be able to see color in the natural object but will often be unwilling to use it in their art work.

10-3

Specific Skills and Concepts To Be Learned:

1. Leaves turn bright colors in autumn.
2. Leaf shapes can be traced with chalk, and painted in with bright colors.

Adaptations:

This is basically an introductory activity. Older children, however, can create an overlapped design of leaves, with the veins carefully drawn in with a black felt-tipped marker.

LESSON 4: SPATTERED COLOR!
DECORATE A SHOPPING BAG WITH COLOR DOTS

Spatter painting creates unusual shopping bags, in which children can carry their school books.

Tools, Materials and Equipment:

Tempera paint	Juice cans
Small paint brushes	Clothespins
Newspaper	Cord
Shopping bags	

Preparation:

1. Pour paint into juice cans. Keep the process simple for young children by using only two colors, such as blue and orange. (One set of two colors for each two children will be sufficient.)
2. Have children put their names on the inside of their shopping bags. (Figure 10-4.)
3. Cover desk and floors around the room with newspapers. Put up cords for hanging wet bags. Clothespins will hold them. (Figure 10-5.)

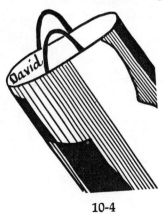

10-4

10-5

4. Be sure children are in smocks, sleeves rolled up (under smocks), and floor well covered. THIS CAN BE A MESSY ACTIVITY.

Developmental Procedure for Activity:

Suggest that children share paintbrushes and work in pairs sharing two colors of paint. One brush should be with the blue paint, and one with the orange.

Place bags on desks. Dip brush into paint, and flip it so that the paint spatters onto the bag. Keep spattering until satisfied with the effect on the shopping bag. (Figure 10-6.) Then turn over and spatter the other side. Hang up to dry.

10-6

Specific Skills and Concepts To Be Learned:

1. Spatter painting makes an attractively colored shopping bag.
2. Paint spatters when a paint brush is flipped.
3. Two colors are adequate to create a design.

Adaptations:

A fine experience for all age levels, it can also be used as a stencilling activity, with a construction paper shape placed on the bag and spattering done all around it. It is, then, carefully moved to another place and spattering is continued. (Figure 10-7.)

LESSON 5: SUGGESTIVE COLOR! USE DRIPPY, BLENDING COLORS

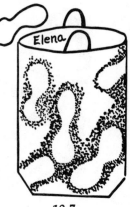

10-7

Colors are cooperative. They seem to blend, join each other and have fun on the very wet surface of the paper.

Tools, Materials and Equipment:

Paint brushes	Felt-tipped markers
Basin	Crayons
Water containers	Tempera paint
Newspaper	Drawing paper, 12" x 18"

Preparation:

Discuss warm and cool colors. Warm colors are like those seen in fire and sun. Cool ones are those seen in water, grass, sky and ice.

A simple demonstration should be given whereby the teacher instructs the child in the following activities.

Developmental Procedure for Activity:

1. Dip the sheet of paper into a wide basin and place on desks where it should be smoothed onto the newspaper. (Figure 10-8.)

2. Decide which type of colors will be used. Will it be warm or cool? Use only one kind, i.e., all red, orange, brown, yellow OR all blue, green, blue-purple, but not a combination of warm and cool.

3. Apply paint by letting the various colors drop (Figure 10-9), or place the brush on the wet surface and the color will seem to be pulled from the brush. (Figure 10-10).

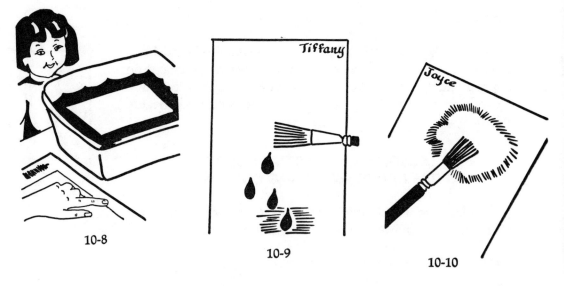

10-8

10-9

10-10

4. See what happens to the colors as they are bled into the water. What does the effect do to the colors as they intermingle? Does the effect suggest sunny skies, a sunset, a storm, fog, or even a fire? Or a stormy sea? LET THE PAINTING BE SUGGESTIVE. What does it suggest to you?

5. Allow paintings to dry thoroughly and then add felt marker or crayon lines to carry out whatever you see in the painting. (Figure 10-11.) (The very young child DOES NOT have to do this part of the activity. He may stop when the painting looks finished.)

Specific Skills and Concepts To Be Learned:

1. Paint can be applied to very wet paper.
2. Colors will bleed into and blend with other colors when they are dropped onto wet paper.
3. Accidental paintings often suggest realistic pictures.

10-11

Adaptations:

Older children can carry out a detailed landscape suggested by the dropped colors. They may apply more paint after the blended colors have dried.

LESSON 6: TRANSPARENT COLOR DISCOS! MAKE SEE-THROUGH COLOR DESIGNS

Transparent designs are see-through designs. A window is transparent, i.e., one can see through it.

Tools, Materials and Equipment:

Scissors	Clear plastic
White glue	Cellophane or colored plastic

Preparation:

Show the children a piece of plastic or cellophane that is transparent. Have them look through each piece and discover what they can see. Search the room for transparent objects. (Bottles, jars, windows, pencil cases, aquariums.)

Developmental Procedure for Activity:

1. Cut two pieces of clear plastic (4" x 4") for each child. (Clear plastic can be salvaged from some gift box tops.)
2. Cut up small snips of cellophane in different colors and

glue onto one piece of clear plastic. Let dry and then glue other piece of clear plastic on top. (Figure 10-12.)

Specific Skills and Concepts To Be Learned:

1. Transparent objects are those you can see through.
2. Colors can be transparent.

Adaptations:

Glue clear scraps of glass (for older children) or scrap plastic to make a see-through design.

10-12

LESSON 7: TRANSLUCENT CIRCLETS!
MAKE SIMULATED STAINED GLASS
WITH TISSUE AND WAX PAPER

The word "translucent" refers to the concept of allowing light to pass through an object. Stained glass is usually translucent as are some plastics and even tissue paper.

Tools, Materials and Equipment:

Tissue paper	Typing paper
Scissors	Ink
Wax paper	Brush
Electric iron	

Preparation:

Precut colored 5″ diameter circles of tissue paper in various colors and 6″ circles of wax paper. Three tissue and four wax paper will be required for each child.

Developmental Procedure for Activity:

Demonstrate translucency:

1. Draw a simple design with ink and a brush on one side of a square of typing paper. Let dry. Turn over.
2. Do a different design on other side. Let dry.
3. Hold up to window or light and note the interesting

results. (You should be able to see both designs together.) Note, too, that you cannot see through this paper as in those used in the previous lesson.

4. Show children that tissue and wax paper are translucent, too. Light passes through both papers.

Proceed to make a translucent circlet as follows:

1. Let child select three tissue circles. They can be all different colors.

2. Instruct children to fold in half, then fold again, and again. (Figure 10-13.)

3. Cut deeply into both folded edges. Unfold and you have a snowflake-like design. Repeat with the three circles. (Figure 10-14.) Save tissue scraps for next lesson.

4. Give four wax paper circles to each child and have them place a wax paper circle, a tissue, a wax, a tissue, etc. until all tissues are between wax paper. (Figure 10-15.)

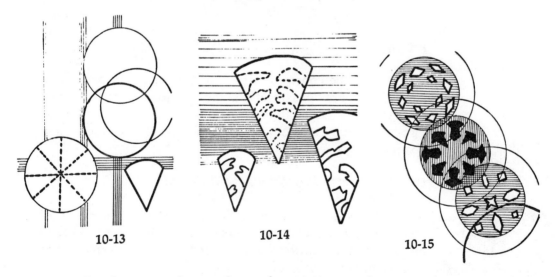

10-13   10-14   10-15

5. Put the wax and tissue designs between newsprint paper and press with a warm iron. The circlets will be welded together in a stiff translucent circle.

Specific Skills and Concepts To Be Learned:

1. Some objects are translucent.
2. They allow light to go through their surface, but we cannot see through them.

Adaptations:

Try stretching some crepe paper. Then hold up to the light. Is it translucent?

Where else can you find the quality of translucency?

LESSON 8: OPACITIES!
MAKING OPAQUE COLOR DESIGNS

The word "opaque" means that one cannot see through the surface of an object. A wall of a building is opaque. A rock is opaque. I'm opaque and so are you!

Tools, Materials and Equipment:

Construction paper   Scissors
White glue   Tissue scraps
Masking tape or wire

Preparation:

Review the concepts of translucency and transparency as developed in previous lessons. Discuss opaque items and search for examples. Look at construction paper. You cannot see through it, nor can you see light through it. Therefore, it is opaque.

Developmental Procedure for Activity:

Cut 5" squares of construction paper. Glue on some of the tiny tissue scraps, left over from previous activity. Test designs by holding them up to the light. Can you see through them? Does light come through?

Turn over and make another design on the other side. Hold up to the light and test again for opacity. (Figure 10-16.)

Fasten to the window with tape or hang from a wire.

10-16

Specific Skills and Concepts To Be Learned:

1. Objects are opaque when you cannot see through them, nor can light come through their surfaces.
2. A test for opacity is to hold an object up to the light.

Adaptations:

Painting on glass scraps or on plastic would be an interesting project for the older children. Or paint on jars, bottles or glasses. Is the paint transparent, translucent or opaque? (There are various paints available for painting on glass. Stains and acrylics are mainly used.)

Cut out a circle from a styrofoam meat tray. Would this be transparent, translucent or opaque? Paint or decorate it.

LESSON 9: CHANGING HUES!
MIXING PRIMARY COLORS INTO SECONDARIES

Colors are called hues, or in other words, colors have names, like red, yellow, blue, orange, green, and violet. The first three are primaries; the second three are secondaries. Mix any two primaries together and the result is a secondary color. That is the message of this lesson.

Tools, Materials and Equipment:

Glasses or jars	Water containers
Crayons	Tempera paint—red,
Newspaper	yellow and blue
Paint brushes	Drawing paper 9" x 12"
	Black felt-tipped markers

Preparation:

The primary colors are those that cannot be mixed. They must be purchased, in their pure form, already mixed in tubes, cakes, jars or bottles. *Red, yellow and blue are primary colors.*

Secondary colors are those made by mixing any two primaries. Blue and yellow make green. Red and blue make violet. Yellow and red make orange. *Orange, green and violet, therefore, are secondary colors.*

In this lesson, color mixing activities are presented mainly for children in grades two and three, not for the very young child.

Developmental Procedure for Activity:

Begin with an exercise using the primary colors. Select red, yellow, and blue crayons and draw giant raindrops. Make them all over the paper, with a crayon. Then fill in a red raindrop, a blue one, a yellow one. Continue until you have a page of brightly colored, primary colored raindrops. Fill in all the in-between space with black felt markers or black crayons. (Figure 10-17.)

10-17

The teacher now becomes a magician and makes colors change:

1. Fill three glasses with watered-down red, yellow and blue tempera paint.

2. Pour some red and some blue together in another glass to demonstrate the making of violet.

3. Pour red and yellow together for orange.

4. Pour yellow and blue together for green.

5. STRESS: ANY TWO PRIMARIES MIXED TOGETHER BECOME A SECONDARY.

Follow with another activity whereby the children are given the chance to do their own color mixing (which will occur as the result of color blending.)

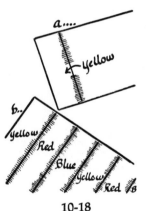

10-18

1. Use your brush and paint the whole sheet of paper with a good coating of water.

2. Now paint a wide strip of yellow paint. (Figure 10-18a.) Next to the yellow, paint another wide band of red . . . then blue . . . and then yellow . . . (Figure 10-18b.)

The colors will blend and run together, making new colors . . . . .SECONDARIES.

Specific Skills and Concepts To Be Learned:

1. Primary colors are red, yellow and blue.
2. Secondary colors are orange, green and violet.
3. Primary colors must be purchased while secondaries can be mixed or purchased.
4. Any two primary colors mixed together will make a secondary.

Adaptations:

Older children may mix many variations of colors in jars, or on a palette.

LESSON 10: MYSTERIOUS SPINNERS!
MAKING DISCS THAT WILL SUGGEST
THAT COLORS CAN APPEAR AND DISAPPEAR

Color is fascinating and mysterious. Colors change when light changes. In this lesson, spinners can be made that will show colors can disappear and reappear. Why?

Tools, Materials and Equipment:

Crayons   White cardboard
Paste   Pencil with eraser
Scissors   Straight pins
Felt markers   Cardboard strips ¼" x 3"

Preparation:

Cut cardboard circles and strips in various sizes as required in each of the following activities.

Developmental Procedure for Activity:

Vanishing Colors:

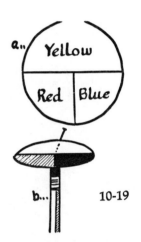

1. Cut out a circular disc from cardboard. Color it with the primary colors: top half in yellow; lower left quarter red, lower right quarter blue. (Figure 10-19a.)
2. Push a pin through the center and push point of pin into the eraser of a pencil. (Figure 10-19b.)
3. Use your fingers to make the circle spin or spin as you would a top. As the disc spins, the colors will blend and disappear.

Changing Colors:

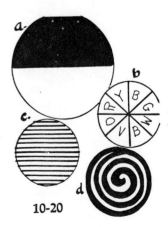

1. Cut out several 3" (diameter) circles from cardboard. Color each differently in any of the following ways:
   A. Fill in with solid colors.
   B. Make half white and half black. (Figure 10-20a.)
   C. Color eight pie sections with primaries and secondaries, plus black and white. (Figure 10-20b.)
   D. Striped design . . . in black and white . . . or in colors (Figure 10-20c)
   E. Spiral design . . . in black and white . . . or in colors. (Figure 10-20d.)

2. Attach to pin, eraser and pencil. Spin and see what happens.

Changing Shapes:

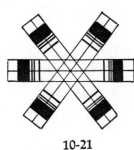

10-21

1. Use three cardboard strips and glue together to make a strip star shape. Color in strip as shown in Figure 10-21.

2. Place on smooth surface and spin fast. What happens? The strips become a circle with circular stripes of color.

Specific Skills and Concepts To Be Learned:

1. Color changes in light.
2. Spinning colors can cause changes in, loss of, or addition to, color.

Adaptations:

More complex experiments may be performed by older children. Young children must stay with the simply made and easily moved designs. Just let them enjoy color (and be learning by osmosis at the same time).

Teaching Arts and Crafts Through Creative Activities

In this, the final section of this book, stress is again placed on being inventive, and imaginative, and working cooperatively.

PART
4

11

Using Inventive
and Imaginative Experiences

Young children want to be entertained. They're growing up with a television set that is almost a member of the family. Mr. T.V. teaches them, makes them laugh, tells them what to eat and what gifts to select. Teachers find it difficult to compete with this extraordinarily versatile robot, but compete they must! How? One way is by introducing a new use for everyday materials.

Help your children invent new uses for materials that are not always regarded as art media or try using art media in a new way. Two examples are presented in this chapter: painting with Epsom salts and chalk drawing in tempera goo. Can you come up with other different activities? Could you make pictures with wood shavings? Button designs? Make an oil painting by combining salad oil and tempera? Brainstorm with your children and you'll have TONS of ideas!

LESSON 1: PAINT WITH EPSOM SALTS!
MAKING SPARKLING PAINTINGS

Epsom salts, a crystalline white powder, is mainly used for medicinal purposes. In this lesson, however, it becomes an art medium.

Tools, Materials and Equipment:

Epsom salts	Used greeting or post cards
Cardboard	Wooden spoon
Hot water	Containers for salt solution
Pot	White glue
Paint brushes	Construction paper
Tissue or shelf paper	

Preparation:

Make a solution of Epsom Salts and very hot water. Add the salts slowly to the water until no more crystals will dissolve. Stir constantly with wooden spoon.

Developmental Procedure for Activity:

On colored construction paper, paint a picture or design using the Epsom salts solution.(Appropriate themes might be: snowflakes, snow people, storms, abstract designs.)

At first, the painting will look like plain, wet paper but when dry, sparkling crystals will appear. Glue onto a contrasting colored background. (Figure 11-1.)

11-1

Specific Skills and Concepts To Be Learned:

1. Epsom salts can be used as an art medium.
2. When water evaporates from an Epsom salts painting, a crystalline picture will emerge.

Adaptations:

Try bath salts. Does it work the same? Or ordinary table salt? . . . invent . . . invent!

Try using a greeting or post card. Cut into an interesting shape. Cover with diluted white glue and let dry. Then paint sections with Epsom salts solution. How does it look?

LESSON 2: TEMPERA GOO!
PAINT WITH SLIPPERY TEMPERA AND CHALK

Mix up a batch of goo by combining paint and glue.

Tools, Materials and Equipment:

Chalk	White tempera paint
Cardboard	Wheat paste
Newspapers	Paint and chalk containers
Plastic spoons	

Preparation:

Prepare two cups of wheat paste according to the manufacturer's directions. Mix this with two cups of white tempera, and pour into small containers, one for every two children. Place a plastic spoon in each.

Put colored chalk in another set of small containers. (It's best to use old chalk, since it will get very SLOPPY.)

Developmental Procedure for Activity:

Apply several heaping spoons of TEMPERA GOO to the cardboard. Spread it around with your hand, as you do with fingerpaint. (Figure 11-2.)

11-2

Draw into the GOO with chalk, drawing right on the wet surface. Use sides as well as the ends of the chalk and use plenty of colors. What happens to the color? It changes, merging with the white paint.

Don't plan your painting, just put some color here, and some there. Before you know it, you'll have an exciting picture or design.

Specific Skills and Concepts To Be Learned:

1. Paint and wheat paste can be combined.
2. Chalk dissolves in water.

Adaptations:

The following are interesting variations on this lesson:

1. Draw with chalk into a wheat paste solution, instead of drawing into the TEMPERA GOO. How is it different?

2. Draw with chalk into a light-colored finger paint, such as yellow.

3. Draw with chalk on a wet surface. (Wet the paper with plain water, or even milk.)

These experiences are of value to children throughout the elementary school.

12

Experiences for Working Together

Social development is vital to the total education of the child. Chapter 12 presents some activities for learning TOGETHERNESS.

LESSON 1: TOY SOLDIER PARADE!
MAKE PATRIOTIC TOY SOLDIERS' HATS

Little children, wearing toy soldiers' hats, can parade around the room, or be a part of a class performance on the stage.

Tools, Materials and Equipment:

Construction paper: red, white, blue and black
Metallic paper: gold
Scissors   Paste
Stapler   Paper clips, two per child

Preparation:

Discuss the differences in the textures of construction paper and metallic paper. One is thick; the other thin. One is slick and smooth. One reflects; the other does not.

Cut paper into exact sizes to be used:

Color	Size	Number of Pieces (Per Child)
Blue	9" x 12"	2
Black	2" x 4½"	1
Red	1" x 9"	3

Color	Size	Number of Pieces (Per Child)
White	1½" x 9"	2
Gold	¾" x 9"	2
White	1½" x 9"	1
Gold	¾" x 9"	1

Developmental Procedure for Activity:

Paper should be passed out as it is used, to lessen confusion.

1. Attach two sheets of blue paper on the 9" side. (Figure 12-1.)

2. Round off the edges of the black paper on two sides for the visor and paste in the middle, at the lower edge of the blue rectangle. (Figure 12-2.)

3. Pass out one white strip and paste over seam. Pass out single gold strip and paste in the middle of the white one. (Figure 12-3.)

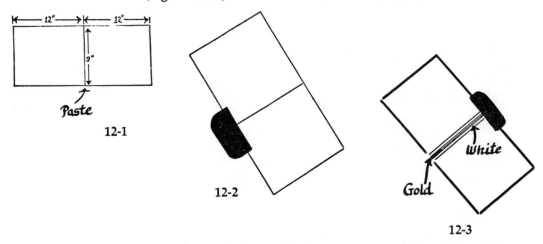

12-1

12-2

White

Gold

12-3

4. Pass out the three red strips and paste each into a loop. Then paste the three together. (Figure 12-4a.) Paste the plume in the middle of the top edge of the visor. (Figure 12-4b.)

5. Pass out two white strips and paste at lower edge - one on the right and one on the left. Paste on top of visor and plume. (Figure 12-5a.)

6. Pass out two strips of gold. Paste in the middle of the white strips. (Figure 12-5b.)

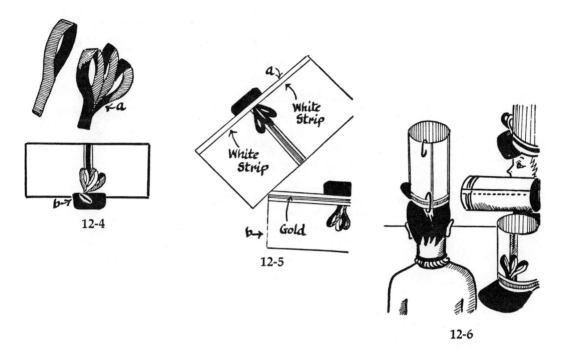

12-4

12-5

12-6

7. Fit hat to child's head by attaching in back with two paper clips. After fitted correctly, staple together at top and bottom. (Figure 12-6.)

Play a march and let children have a parade of THE TOY SOLDIERS.

Specific Skills and Concepts To Be Learned:

1. Papers have different textures.
2. Putting different textures together makes an interesting hat.
3. Marching together is fun.

Adaptations:

This lesson is basically for the kindergarten and primary child but it can be used for costuming when the older child has to dress up for Halloween or a school play.

Color schemes can be changed, i.e., try a red and green hat for Christmas. Put on holly leaves instead of a plume, or even make a small cut paper Santa Claus and paste on the front.

LESSON 2: CUT UP SCENERY!
CREATE SIMPLE MODERN DESIGN SCENERY
FOR A PLAY OR MUSICAL

Young children often find it difficult to know where reality ends and imagination begins. They enjoy daydreaming, or thinking that the impossible is true. So . . . why not let them dream up a play . . . and construct very simple scenery and stage properties that even they can do.

Tools, Materials and Equipment:

Scissors	Tempera paint
Brushes	Large boxes
Paint containers	Pins
Construction paper	Staplers
String	

Preparation:

Dream up a play. Decide what music, if any, will be sung. Have fun with it . . . keep it exciting and informal. Let it fall into place by itself. Discuss what scenery is needed. KEEP IT SIMPLE!

If possible, arrange to have the back wall of the stage covered with Celotex corkboard, or a similar material. Have custodians paint it a neutral color, or light blue (since a sky background is so often used.) With this kind of back wall, cut paper scenery can be stapled or tacked into place.

Developmental Procedure for Activity:

Cut out large geometrical or free-form shapes from construction paper (24" x 36"). These can be used as follows:

1. Punch holes in them, attach string in holes and hang from the teasers. (Teasers are the overhead curtains attached to the stage ceiling.) (Figure 12-7.)
2. Pin shapes to the side curtains. (Figure 12-8.)
3. Attach shapes to the back wall. Use lots of them; overlapping; placing colors on top of other colors. Let accidental designs happen by overlapping shapes. Then step back . . .

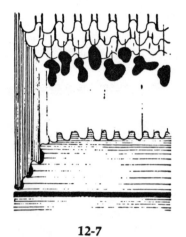

12-7

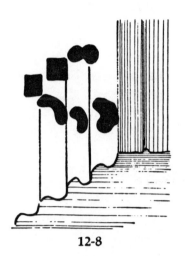

12-8

12-9

and see what you have. Add another shape. Does it look better now? (Figure 12-9.)

4. Ripple some shapes to get a three-dimensional effect. (Figure 12-10.)

Paint huge boxes in bright colors to be used as tables and benches (if strong enough) or just use them for decoration. (Figure 12-11.)

12-10

12-11

Specific Skills and Concepts To Be Learned:

1. Free forms and geometrical shapes can be used to create scenery for a play or musical.
2. Large boxes, brightly painted, can be used as stage properties.
3. Shapes can be hung from the teasers.
4. Teasers are the overhead curtains from the stage ceiling.

Adaptations:

Older children may make extensive designs for a stage show using more planning skills.

LESSON 3: SWIRLING COLOR!
USING THE OVERHEAD PROJECTOR
TO CREATE MOVING COLOR

The overhead projector is another wonderful tool to use in learning about color. It is also used as another TOGETHERNESS ACTIVITY.

Tools, Materials and Equipment:

Overhead projector and screen	Sponges
Shallow dish (transparent)	Vegetable oil
	Tempera paint
Food coloring	Water
Clothespins (clamp type)	Egg
	Prism
Drawing paper, 12" x 18"	
Flat piece of clear glass	
Reproductions of Jackson Pollock paintings	

Preparation:

Look at a glass prism and notice how it breaks up white light into a rainbow of colors. Also, look at and discuss the colors seen in rainbows, oily puddles, soap bubbles, and the sun coming into the room through a fish aquarium.

Developmental Procedure for Activity:

Discover the beauty of colors by looking at them with the overhead projector. Set up projector and screen and try the following learning experiences:

Activity No. 1:

1. Place a low, flat, clear glass dish on an overhead projector. Partially fill with water.
2. Break an egg into water and stir. (Figure 12-12.)
3. What do you see on the screen?

12-12

12-13

Activity No. 2:

1. Place a piece of flat glass on the projector.
2. Put some drops of oil on the glass (Figure 12-13a) then some tempera spots, and place another piece of flat glass on top of oil and paint. (Figure 12-13b.) Squeeze glass together.
3. What do you see on the screen?
4. Try more oil and paint and another piece of glass on top. What occurs now?

Activity No. 3:

At this point some nonrepresentational art can be introduced. Look at a Jackson Pollock painting and discover similarities to the overhead projector swirl designs. What colors are in the Pollock painting? What colors are in the swirl designs?

Activity No. 4:

1. Place the low, flat, clear glass dish on the projector. Pour vegetable oil into the dish, just covering the bottom.

2. Add a small amount of food coloring (one color only). Watch the screen. What's happening? Does the color mix with the oil? No, it forms into bubbles.

3. Now pour just enough water in to burst the color bubbles.

4. Have a child move the dish gently. What happens? The color will burst into glorious beauty as it is projected on the wall.

5. Continue shaking and see what happens. Add new colors, too.

Activity No. 5:

Now create your own painting of swirling color. Attach small pieces of sponge to a clip-handled clothespin. The clothespin becomes the handle for a sponge-brush. (Figure 12-14.)

Dip the sponge into paint and paint swirls on drawing paper. Clean sponge brush and try another color. Keep painting brilliant swirls all over the paper.

12-14

Specific Skills and Concepts To Be Learned:

1. An overhead projector can make accidental but temporary wall paintings.
2. Oil and water do not mix. Hence, oil and water-based colors do not mix.
3. Food coloring and tempera paint are water-based colors.
4. Jackson Pollock made paintings with swirling colors.

Adaptations:

All of these experiences are fun and good learning experiences throughout the elementary school. THEY PROMOTE TOGETHERNESS, also.

Older children, of course, can become more experimental with the overhead projector wall painting.

LESSON 4: COLOR GAMES!
THE FUN WAY TO LEARN ABOUT COLOR

Learn all about color by working (and playing) together.

Tools, Materials and Equipment:

Colored chalk	Drawing paper
Scissors	Boxes
Drawing paper	Pencils
Construction paper	White glue
Cardboard	Envelopes
Felt-tipped markers	Reproductions of paintings

The children will find the following color games to be most enjoyable.

Color Ring:

Children join hands, form a circle and walk around in a circle. One child is selected as the leader and is stationed inside the ring. He calls out: "Colors, colors, colors! Sit down if you are wearing the color . . . . . . red!" Everyone with a piece of red clothing sits down.

The circle forms again. Then he calls out "Colors, colors, colors. Sit down if you are wearing the color . . . . . . yellow." All those wearing yellow sit down.

This process is continued until all of the primary (red, yellow and blue) and all but one of the secondaries (green, orange and violet) have been used. The child (or children) left become(s) the new leader(s).

Color Masterpieces:

Collect reproductions of famous paintings whose titles include a color. (Some possibilities are: Thomas Gainsborough's *Blue Boy;* Jim Dine's *Five Toothbrushes on Black Ground;* Jules Olitski's *High a Yellow;* Mark Rothko's *White and Greens in Blue,* and Alexander Calder's *The Orange Panel.*)

Mount on cardboard and print the name of the painting and the artist on the back, using a felt-tipped marker. Let the children guess the color that is a part of the painting's name.

After becoming acquainted with the paintings, they can play the game themselves, trying to remember the names and artists involved.

I See A Color:

"I see a color; it is blue" says the leader. Children then try to guess what object in the room has blue on it and is the one the leader is referring to. Whoever guesses correctly becomes the next leader. He picks another color, on another object, and the game continues. . .

Color Days:

Have a color day on which everyone will wear a predetermined color. Even the writing on the chalkboard should be done in the color of the day.

Matching Colors:

Make a set of identical shapes; have two of each color. Place one of each color in an envelope and the other of the same color in a box. In other words, there will be a red, yellow, blue, green, orange and violet shape in the box and also a set will be in the envelope.

When playing the game, the child spills out the colors from the envelope onto his desk. He then attempts to match the colors by taking a red from the box to match the red from the envelope.

Color Search:

Divide the class into color teams, giving the people on each team a piece of paper in the correct color. The red team will be given red pieces of construction paper.

Children now walk around the school, listing all the items they can find in their particular color. The team with the most color objects found wins the game.

Team Colors:

Divide class into color teams. Each color team will write all day long with one color. (The green team will write only with green, the red team with red, etc.) Have the class draw pictures, but again *they can use only the color of their team.*

Specific Skills and Concepts To Be Learned:

1. Colors are all around us.
2. Children can cooperate in playing games in order to see colors.

3. Artists use color in the names of their paintings as well as in the paintings themselves.

Adaptations:

These games are introductory and can be used to best advantage in grades kindergarten through three. Older children have already developed their color sense, and therefore should be more involved in the formal use of color.

LESSON 5: CHANGE THE COLORS YOU SEE! MAKING COLORED GLASSES

Play a game similar to "I See A Color" but use colored eye glasses.

Tools, Materials and Equipment:

Pencil	Scissors
Coffee can lid	Colored plastic
Oaktag	Stapler
String or yarn	

Preparation:

Look at a pair of glasses. Discuss the parts and how we can make colored glasses with the materials right here in the classroom. When we wear the glasses we make, all the colors we see will be affected and changed.

Developmental Procedure for Activity:

Have children make their colored eye glasses as follows:

1. Trace around a plastic coffee can lid two times on a sheet of oaktag. Leave a one-inch space between circles, for ease in cutting. (Figure 12-15.)

2. Cut out the two circles. Fold in half and draw one-half smaller circle inside. (Figure 12-16.) Cut on the dotted line and you have two eye glass frames. (Figure 12-17.)

3. Select two pieces of colored plastic. Staple each to the back of a circle frame and cut off excess plastic. (Figure 12-18.)

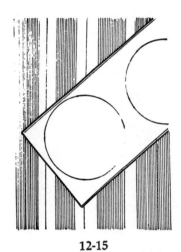

12-15

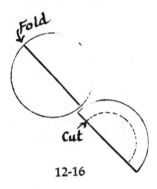

Fold

Cut

12-16

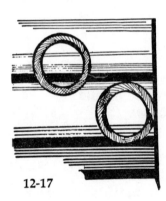

12-17

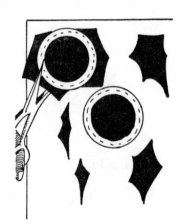

12-18

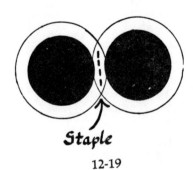

Staple

12-19

Tie

Knot

12-20

4. Staple both frames together in the middle. (Figure 12-19.)

5. Make a hole in the side of each frame. Cut two lengths of string or yarn about ten inches long, and make a knot in the end of each. Insert one string in each side of the glasses. (Figure 12-20.) Tie at the back of the child's head so that he can wear his glasses.

6. What does the new environment look like? The colors are certainly different!

Specific Skills and Concepts To Be Learned:

1. Colors change when we look through colored plastic.

Adaptations:

Instead of making glasses, use a slide made with one color of plastic and insert in a manual slide projector along with a regular slide (showing scenery, painting or piece of sculpture). What happens to a cloud when you see it with a red slide beside it? What happens to Van Gogh's blue sky (in *Starry Night*) when a purple slide is placed beside it?

Index